PARMA
Tour Guide
2025
Vic Harvey

Parma Tour Guide 2025

©2024 by Vic Harvey
All rights reserved.

No part of this publication may be reproduced, distributed, or transmitted in any form or by any means, including photocopying, recording, or other electronic or mechanical methods, without the prior written permission of the publisher, except in the case of brief quotations embodied in critical reviews and certain other noncommercial uses permitted by copyright law.

TABLE OF CONTENT

CHAPTER 1: 8

DISCOVER THE CULINARY DELIGHTS OF PARMA........8
EXPLORE THE RICH FLAVORS THAT MAKE PARMA A GASTRONOMIC PARADISE..8
SAVOR TRADITIONAL DISHES LIKE PROSCIUTTO DI PARMA AND PARMIGIANO REGGIANO 10
UNCOVER LOCAL MARKETS THAT SHOWCASE THE BEST OF ITALIAN INGREDIENTS 13

CHAPTER 2: 17

VISIT ICONIC HISTORICAL SITES...............................17
MARVEL AT THE STUNNING ARCHITECTURE OF THE PALAZZO DELLA PILOTTA..17
DISCOVER THE INTRICATE DETAILS OF THE BAPTISTERY OF PARMA 19
WANDER THROUGH THE IMPRESSIVE CATHEDRAL OF PARMA, A MASTERPIECE OF ART 22

CHAPTER 3: 26

EXPERIENCE PARMA'S VIBRANT ART SCENE 26
EXPLORE THE CAPTIVATING WORKS OF THE FAMOUS ARTIST CORREGGIO..26
VISIT THE GALLERIA NAZIONALE TO SEE RENOWNED ITALIAN MASTERPIECES..29
ENGAGE WITH LOCAL GALLERIES SHOWCASING CONTEMPORARY ART AND TALENT 32

CHAPTER 4: **36**

STROLL THROUGH CHARMING NEIGHBORHOODS ..36
WANDER THE PICTURESQUE STREETS OF THE HISTORIC CITY CENTER 36
DISCOVER HIDDEN SQUARES FILLED WITH LOCAL CAFÉS AND SHOPS 40
EXPERIENCE THE WARM HOSPITALITY OF THE PEOPLE IN QUAINT NEIGHBORHOODS 45

CHAPTER 5: **50**

INDULGE IN PARMA'S SWEET TREATS 50
SATISFY YOUR SWEET TOOTH WITH LOCAL DELICACIES LIKE TORTA FRITTA 50
LEARN ABOUT THE ART OF MAKING TRADITIONAL ITALIAN GELATO 56
VISIT BAKERIES KNOWN FOR THEIR IRRESISTIBLE PASTRIES AND CAKES 61

CHAPTER 6: **65**

RELAX IN BEAUTIFUL PARKS AND GARDENS 65
ENJOY A LEISURELY AFTERNOON IN THE PARCO DUCALE 65
DISCOVER THE LUSH GREENERY AND TRANQUIL ATMOSPHERE OF GIARDINO DELLA GHIARA 68
ENGAGE IN OUTDOOR ACTIVITIES WHILE SOAKING UP THE ITALIAN SUN 70

CHAPTER 7: **74**

ATTEND LOCAL FESTIVALS AND EVENTS 74
EXPERIENCE THE EXCITEMENT OF THE ANNUAL FIERA DI SAN GIOVANNI 74

Join The Celebrations Of The Festival Of Prosciutto Di Parma..77
Discover Cultural Events That Showcase Parma's Rich Heritage 81

CHAPTER 8: 86

EXPLORE THE SURROUNDING COUNTRYSIDE 86
Take A Scenic Drive Through The Stunning Emilia-Romagna Region 86
Visit Vineyards Producing World-Renowned Wines Like Lambrusco 91
Experience The Charm Of Small Villages That Dot The Countryside 93

CHAPTER 9: 97

DISCOVER THE REGION'S RICH HISTORY 97
Learn About Parma's Role In The Renaissance Period 97
Visit Museums That House Artifacts From Various Historical Eras..100
Explore The Connections Between Parma And Notable Historical Figures 102

CHAPTER 10: 106

SAVOR THE LOCAL WINE SELECTION 106
Indulge In Tastings Of Regional Wines At Local Wineries 106
Learn About The Unique Characteristics Of Parma's Winemaking Process 109
Pair Wines With Local Cheeses For An Authentic Experience 112

5|

CHAPTER 11: 116

    ENGAGE WITH LOCAL ARTISANS............................*116*
    VISIT WORKSHOPS WHERE SKILLED ARTISANS CREATE TRADITIONAL CRAFTS..116
    LEARN ABOUT THE IMPORTANCE OF CRAFTSMANSHIP IN PARMA'S CULTURE..119
    TAKE HOME UNIQUE SOUVENIRS THAT REFLECT THE LOCAL ARTISTRY 122

CHAPTER 12: 126

    EXPLORE UNIQUE SHOPPING EXPERIENCES *126*
    STROLL THROUGH BOUTIQUES OFFERING HANDMADE GOODS AND LOCAL PRODUCTS 126
    DISCOVER ARTISAN MARKETS FEATURING FRESH PRODUCE AND CRAFTS..129
    FIND PERFECT GIFTS THAT CAPTURE THE ESSENCE OF PARMA..133

CHAPTER 13: 137

    YOUR 6-DAY ADVENTURE AWAITS........................*137*
    A WELL-CRAFTED ITINERARY TO MAKE THE MOST OF YOUR STAY IN PARMA..137

CHAPTER 1:

DISCOVER THE CULINARY DELIGHTS OF PARMA

Explore The Rich Flavors That Make Parma A Gastronomic Paradise

Parma, a city nestled in the heart of Italy's Emilia-Romagna region, is renowned for its rich culinary heritage that captivates food lovers from all corners of the globe. The city's gastronomy is not just about the dishes; it is a celebration of history, tradition, and local ingredients that come together to create a unique flavor profile. One of the best ways to experience this culinary paradise is by indulging in its traditional offerings and understanding the cultural significance behind them.

From the first bite of Prosciutto di Parma, you'll understand why this city is a gastronomic jewel. This dry-cured ham is made from carefully selected pigs raised in the Parma region, and the production methods have been passed down through generations. The art of making Prosciutto di Parma begins with the careful selection of the pork leg, which is then salted and aged for a minimum of 12 months. The resulting ham is tender, sweet, and savory, often enjoyed with fresh bread, cheese, or simply on its own.

The Parmigiano Reggiano cheese is another must-try when visiting Parma. Known as the "King of Cheeses," it is crafted using time-honored methods that date back to the Middle Ages. The cheese is made from raw cow's milk, and the aging process can last from 12 months to over 36 months, resulting in a complex flavor that is nutty and slightly crumbly. You can visit local dairies, like Caseificio San Pier Damiani, where you can see the cheese-making process firsthand. Tours typically last about an hour and cost around $15 per person. These experiences often include tastings, allowing you to savor the different aging profiles of Parmigiano Reggiano.

To fully appreciate the culinary landscape of Parma, consider joining a local food tour. Many companies, like Parma Food Tours, offer guided experiences that take you through the city's hidden gems, including family-owned restaurants, artisanal shops, and markets. A typical tour costs about $100 per person and lasts approximately three hours. You'll have the chance to taste a variety of local delicacies, learn about the history of Parma's cuisine, and interact with local chefs and artisans who are passionate about their craft.

Overall, exploring the rich flavors of Parma is not just a meal; it is an experience steeped in history and tradition. Whether you're sampling aged ham, enjoying a piece of cheese, or indulging in a guided food tour, each moment allows you to connect with the culture and heritage of this beautiful city.

Savor Traditional Dishes Like Prosciutto Di Parma And Parmigiano Reggiano

When it comes to the traditional dishes of Parma, few can rival the iconic Prosciutto di Parma and Parmigiano Reggiano. These two staples of Italian cuisine not only define the culinary landscape of the region but also embody the passion and craftsmanship of local producers.

Prosciutto di Parma is a beloved delicacy that is recognized worldwide for its exquisite taste and quality. This ham is made from pigs raised in the Parma region, where they are fed a diet rich in grains and whey, contributing to the ham's distinct flavor. The production of Prosciutto di Parma is a meticulous process that requires time and precision. After the ham is salted and carefully massaged, it is left to age for a minimum of 12 months in a controlled environment that allows the flavors to develop naturally. The result is a ham that melts in your mouth, with a delicate balance of sweetness and saltiness. To truly savor this dish, enjoy it wrapped around melon, paired with a glass of local wine, or served with crusty bread.

Parmigiano Reggiano, often referred to as the "Parmesan," is another cornerstone of Parma's culinary identity. This cheese is produced in the regions of Parma, Reggio

Emilia, Modena, and parts of Bologna and Mantua. The production process is governed by strict regulations, ensuring that only the highest quality cheese is labeled as Parmigiano Reggiano. The cheese is made using raw cow's milk and aged for a minimum of 12 months, with some varieties aged for over 36 months. The aging process contributes to its complex flavor, which ranges from nutty to fruity, with a crystalline texture that makes it perfect for grating over pasta, risottos, or salads.

You can find both Prosciutto di Parma and Parmigiano Reggiano in local trattorias, where they are often served as part of an antipasto platter. One such recommended spot is Trattoria Corrieri, known for its authentic dishes and cozy atmosphere. A meal here typically costs around $30 per person, and the menu includes a selection of cured meats, cheeses, and homemade pasta that showcases the region's culinary heritage.

If you want a more hands-on experience, consider taking a cooking class focused on these traditional dishes. Local chefs offer classes where you can learn how to prepare pasta from scratch, pair it with homemade sauces, and create authentic Italian dishes featuring Prosciutto and Parmigiano. Classes usually cost between $80 and $150 per person and typically last around three hours, providing an immersive culinary experience that will enhance your appreciation of these local specialties.

In summary, savoring traditional dishes like Prosciutto di Parma and Parmigiano Reggiano is a must when visiting the city. Each bite tells a story of craftsmanship and heritage, allowing you to connect with the essence of Parma's culinary tradition.

Uncover Local Markets That Showcase The Best Of Italian Ingredients

To truly experience the culinary culture of Parma, a visit to the local markets is essential. These vibrant hubs of activity not only offer a plethora of fresh ingredients but also provide insight into the daily lives of the locals and their gastronomic practices. The markets are a feast for the senses, bursting with colors, aromas, and the lively chatter of vendors and shoppers alike.

One of the most popular markets in Parma is Mercato di Piazza Ghiaia, a lively market that operates on Tuesdays, Thursdays, and Saturdays. This market is known for its wide variety of fresh produce, meats, cheeses, and artisanal products. Here, you can find local farmers showcasing their seasonal fruits and vegetables, often harvested that very morning. You can stroll through the stalls, sample fresh cheeses, and chat with the friendly vendors who are eager to share their knowledge about their products. The market opens early in the morning, around 7:00 AM, and typically closes around 1:00 PM, making it a perfect morning outing for food enthusiasts.

Another must-visit market is Mercato Coperto, located in the heart of the city. This covered market is open every day and offers an array of local products, from cured meats and cheeses to homemade pasta and baked goods. The market is an excellent place to discover traditional delicacies, including truffles, seasonal vegetables, and regional wines. You can also enjoy a leisurely breakfast at one of the small cafés within the market, where you can sip a cappuccino while indulging in a freshly baked pastry. Prices at the Mercato Coperto vary, but you can expect to pay around $5 for coffee and pastry.

For a unique experience, consider joining a local market tour. These tours often include tastings of various products and insights into the culinary traditions of the region. They typically last around two hours and cost approximately $60 per person. This immersive experience allows you to learn about local ingredients, engage with vendors, and understand how to select the best products for your cooking.

When visiting these markets, be sure to bring a reusable bag to carry your purchases. Local markets not only provide a chance to sample and buy fresh ingredients but also foster a sense of community, allowing you to interact with the locals and gain a deeper understanding of Parma's culinary identity.

In conclusion, uncovering the local markets of Parma is an essential part of your culinary journey. These markets are the heartbeat of the city, showcasing the finest Italian ingredients and offering a unique glimpse into the region's vibrant food culture. By exploring the markets, you not only fill your basket with delightful treats but also enrich your experience in this gastronomic paradise.

CHAPTER 2:

VISIT ICONIC HISTORICAL SITES

Marvel At The Stunning Architecture Of The Palazzo Della Pilotta

The Palazzo della Pilotta is one of Parma's most significant architectural landmarks, a stunning example of Renaissance design that captures the city's rich cultural heritage. Nestled in the heart of Parma, this grand palace complex is a testament to the power and prestige of the Farnese family, who commissioned its construction in the late 16th century. As you approach the Palazzo, you are greeted by its imposing façade, characterized by a mix of architectural styles that reflect the evolving tastes of the time.

Originally built to serve as the residence for the Farnese dukes, the Palazzo della Pilotta has undergone numerous transformations throughout its history. Today, it houses several important institutions, including the National Gallery, the Farnese Theatre, and the Archaeological Museum. Each section of the Palazzo offers a unique glimpse into Parma's artistic and cultural past, making it an essential stop for any visitor.

The highlight of the Palazzo is undoubtedly the Teatro Farnese, an exquisite wooden theatre constructed in 1618, renowned for its elaborate stage design and exceptional acoustics. This remarkable structure was built entirely of wood, showcasing the craftsmanship of the period. The theatre has a capacity of about 300 spectators and is often used for special performances and events, allowing visitors to experience the magic of live theater in a historic setting. The best way to appreciate the theatre is to catch a performance, which typically lasts about two hours. Ticket prices vary depending on the event, usually ranging from $20 to $50.

The Palazzo also features a vast courtyard that is perfect for leisurely strolls. Here, you can soak in the ambiance of this historic site while admiring the intricate details of the surrounding architecture. The courtyard is surrounded by impressive columns and features various sculptures that narrate stories of Parma's illustrious past. The Palazzo opens daily at 9:00 AM, and a typical visit lasts around two to three hours. Admission fees vary by section; for example, entry to the National Gallery is approximately $10, which grants access to a stunning collection of paintings, including works by Correggio and Parmigianino.

In conclusion, marveling at the stunning architecture of the Palazzo della Pilotta offers a captivating journey through Parma's rich history and artistic legacy. The blend of Renaissance artistry and cultural significance makes this landmark a must-see for anyone visiting the city. Make sure to take your time to explore the various museums and enjoy the beauty of the architectural elements that surround you.

Discover The Intricate Details Of The Baptistery Of Parma

The Baptistery of Parma is an architectural gem that showcases the artistry and religious significance of the city. Located next to the

Cathedral of Parma, this striking octagonal structure was constructed between 1196 and 1270 and is considered one of the finest examples of Romanesque architecture in Italy. Its pink Verona marble façade, adorned with intricate carvings and sculptures, draws the eye of every passerby, inviting them to explore its rich history.

As you approach the Baptistery, take a moment to admire its stunning exterior. The façade is adorned with beautifully carved reliefs that depict biblical scenes and figures, showcasing the exceptional craftsmanship of medieval artisans. The entrance, framed by a grand portal, features a detailed sculpture of the Last Judgment, serving as a reminder of the building's religious purpose. The intricacies of the carvings reflect the theological and cultural ideals of the time, offering a glimpse into the medieval mindset and devotion.

Upon entering the Baptistery, you are immediately struck by the ethereal beauty of its interior. The dome is adorned with exquisite frescoes painted by the renowned artist Correggio in the early 16th century, depicting scenes from the life of Christ and various saints. These captivating images are not only a testament to Correggio's skill but also to the spiritual significance of the Baptistery as a place of worship. The play of light within the dome creates a mesmerizing atmosphere, enhancing the spiritual experience for visitors.

The Baptistery is also home to several beautiful sculptures and altars, each with its unique story and significance. One of the most notable features is the large baptismal font located at the center of the building. This marble font, intricately carved and adorned with reliefs, has been the site of countless baptisms since the Baptistery's inception. It symbolizes the beginning of the Christian journey, welcoming new members into the faith.

Visiting the Baptistery is not just about admiring its architectural beauty; it is also an opportunity to connect with the spiritual and historical essence of Parma. The site is open daily from 9:00 AM to 7:00 PM, allowing ample time for exploration. Admission fees are modest, typically around $6, making it accessible for all visitors. Guided tours are also available, providing deeper insights into the artwork and historical significance of the Baptistery.

In summary, discovering the intricate details of the Baptistery of Parma is a journey into the heart of the city's spiritual heritage. The remarkable artistry, rich history, and serene atmosphere make this site an essential part of your visit to Parma. Whether you are an art enthusiast, a history buff, or simply seeking a peaceful moment of reflection, the Baptistery promises an unforgettable experience.

Wander Through The Impressive Cathedral Of Parma, A Masterpiece Of Art

The Cathedral of Parma, officially known as the Cattedrale di Santa Maria Assunta, is an architectural masterpiece that stands as a testament to the city's rich artistic heritage. Located adjacent to the Baptistery, this magnificent structure showcases a blend of Romanesque and Gothic styles, creating a visually stunning representation of religious architecture. The Cathedral was built between 1059 and 1178, making it one of the oldest churches in Parma.

As you approach the Cathedral, the façade immediately captures your attention with its intricate carvings and impressive rose window. The façade is adorned with statues of saints and biblical figures, adding to its grandeur. The towering bell tower, known as the Campanile, rises majestically above the surrounding buildings, inviting visitors to explore its interior. As you enter, the sheer scale of the Cathedral takes your breath away, with its soaring arches and vaulted ceilings creating a sense of awe and reverence.

One of the Cathedral's most notable features is the stunning fresco that adorns the dome, painted by the acclaimed artist Correggio in the 16th century. This masterpiece, known as "Assumption of the Virgin," depicts the Virgin Mary being taken up to heaven, surrounded by a host of angels and saints. The use of light and shadow in the fresco creates a dynamic sense of movement, drawing the viewer's eye upward. The vibrant colors and intricate details showcase Correggio's exceptional talent, making this artwork a highlight of your visit.

Within the Cathedral, you will also find beautiful chapels, each with its unique artwork and historical significance. The Chapel of the Holy Sacrament features exquisite Baroque decorations and stunning altarpieces, while the Chapel of Saint John the Evangelist houses a remarkable wooden crucifix. Each chapel invites contemplation and reflection, allowing visitors to immerse themselves in the spiritual atmosphere of the Cathedral.

The Cathedral of Parma is open to visitors daily from 7:00 AM to 12:00 PM and from 4:00 PM to 7:00 PM. Admission is free, although donations are welcomed to support the ongoing preservation of this architectural treasure. Guided tours are also available for those who wish to delve deeper into the history and artistry of the Cathedral. These tours typically last about an hour and cost around $10 per person, providing valuable insights into the significance of the various artworks and architectural features.

In conclusion, wandering through the impressive Cathedral of Parma is a journey into the heart of the city's artistic legacy. From the breathtaking frescoes to the intricate details of the architecture, every aspect of the Cathedral tells a story of faith, artistry, and history. Whether you are an art lover, a history enthusiast, or simply seeking a moment of tranquility, the Cathedral offers an enriching experience that will leave a lasting impression on your visit to Parma.

CHAPTER 3:

EXPERIENCE PARMA'S VIBRANT ART SCENE

Explore The Captivating Works Of The Famous Artist Correggio

Correggio, born Antonio Allegri in 1489, is one of Italy's most celebrated Renaissance painters, known for his masterful use of light and shadow, as well as his dynamic compositions. His works have left an indelible mark on the art world, and Parma, his birthplace, is home to some of his most significant masterpieces. Exploring Correggio's works provides an opportunity to appreciate not only his artistic genius but also the cultural context in which he created his art.

One of Correggio's most notable contributions is his innovative approach to fresco painting, particularly evident in the dome of the Cathedral of Parma, where his famous work "Assumption of the Virgin" is located. This fresco, completed between 1526 and 1530, is a remarkable example of his ability to create the illusion of three-dimensional space. As you gaze upwards, you'll be captivated by the way the figures seem to float and swirl within the dome, enhanced by the dramatic use of chiaroscuro that gives depth and vitality to the scene. Correggio's skillful blending of figures and architectural elements transforms the dome into a heavenly realm, inviting viewers to experience a sense of divine presence.

Another significant work by Correggio is "Jupiter and Io," housed in the Galleria Nazionale di Parma. This painting captures a moment from classical mythology, depicting the god Jupiter in a moment of passion for the mortal woman Io. The interplay of light on the figures, along with the soft, ethereal quality of the background, exemplifies Correggio's ability to convey emotion and movement. The sensuality and intimacy of the scene highlight his mastery of human anatomy and expression, making it a must-see for art enthusiasts.

To truly appreciate Correggio's impact, consider visiting the Palazzo della Pilotta, where many of his works are displayed. The

National Gallery features a selection of his paintings, allowing visitors to immerse themselves in his artistic evolution. The museum's collection includes "The Holy Night" and "The Madonna with Child and Saint John," each showcasing his distinctive style and emotional depth. You can expect to spend a few hours exploring the gallery, which is open from 9:00 AM to 7:00 PM, with an admission fee of around $10.

Engaging with Correggio's art is more than just viewing paintings; it is an experience that transports you to the Renaissance era. Each piece invites reflection on the themes of divinity, mythology, and human emotion. As you explore these captivating works, you'll gain insights into the cultural and historical influences that shaped Correggio's vision and legacy. Don't miss the chance to appreciate the brilliance of this master artist, whose works continue to inspire and enchant visitors to Parma.

Visit The Galleria Nazionale To See Renowned Italian Masterpieces

The Galleria Nazionale di Parma is a treasure trove of art, showcasing an impressive collection of Italian masterpieces that span several centuries. Located within the Palazzo della Pilotta, the gallery features works by renowned artists such as Parmigianino, Titian, and, of course, Correggio. Visiting this museum is essential for anyone wanting to delve into the rich artistic heritage of Parma and Italy as a whole.

As you step into the Galleria Nazionale, you are greeted by a breathtaking array of paintings, sculptures, and decorative arts. The museum's layout allows for a smooth flow of exploration, with each room presenting a unique theme or period. One of the standout pieces is Parmigianino's "Madonna with the Long Neck," an extraordinary work that exemplifies the Mannerist style. The elongated figures and graceful composition reflect the artist's innovative approach, inviting viewers to appreciate the beauty of form and color. The museum provides informative labels in both Italian and English, enriching your understanding of each artwork.

Another highlight of the collection is Titian's "Mary Magdalen," which captivates with its rich colors and emotional intensity. Titian's ability to portray human feelings and narratives through his brushwork is a testament to his status as one of the leading painters of the Venetian school. As you stand before these masterpieces, you can't help but feel a connection to the artists and their creative processes, understanding the cultural significance of their work in the context of Italian history.

The Galleria Nazionale also hosts temporary exhibitions that further enhance the visitor experience. These exhibitions often feature contemporary artists or focus on specific themes within the realm of Italian art, making each visit unique. It's advisable to check the gallery's official website for current exhibitions and special events, as these can provide additional layers of insight into the art world.

The museum is open every day from 9:00 AM to 7:00 PM, with an admission fee of approximately $10, which is a modest price for the wealth of cultural experience on offer. Guided tours are available for those looking to deepen their engagement with the artworks, often led by knowledgeable curators who can provide fascinating anecdotes and historical context. These tours typically last around 90 minutes, allowing visitors to explore key pieces in detail.

In conclusion, visiting the Galleria Nazionale di Parma is a journey through Italy's artistic legacy. The collection's breadth and depth offer an unparalleled opportunity to appreciate the creativity and craftsmanship of Italian masters. Whether you are an art aficionado or a casual visitor, the Galleria promises to enrich your understanding of Italy's cultural heritage and leave you inspired by the beauty of its art.

Engage With Local Galleries Showcasing Contemporary Art And Talent

While Parma is renowned for its historical art and architecture, the city also has a vibrant contemporary art scene that reflects its dynamic cultural landscape. Engaging with local galleries offers visitors a chance to explore the work of emerging artists and established talents, showcasing a diverse range of mediums and styles. This contemporary art movement is crucial for understanding the evolving identity of Parma and its place in the modern art world.

One prominent gallery to consider visiting is the Galleria Studio N.O.V.A. This space is dedicated to promoting contemporary art and regularly features exhibitions that highlight both local and international artists. The gallery's mission is to provide a platform for innovative and experimental works, allowing visitors to witness the cutting-edge of artistic expression. Opening hours typically run from 10:00 AM to 1:00 PM and from 4:00 PM to

7:00 PM, and entry is usually free, making it accessible for everyone.

Another noteworthy venue is the Centro Studi e Archivio della Comunicazione (CSAC), located at the University of Parma. This unique center focuses on the study of visual communication and contemporary art, housing a vast archive of materials from various artistic disciplines. The CSAC hosts exhibitions, workshops, and events that encourage dialogue about contemporary artistic practices. Exploring the CSAC can provide a deeper understanding of how artists are responding to current societal issues and how their work engages with the public. Regular exhibitions are often accompanied by talks or panel discussions, adding a layer of interactivity to your visit.

As you engage with these galleries, take the time to connect with the artists and curators. Many local galleries offer opportunities for visitors to attend artist talks or studio visits, where you can gain insight into the creative processes and inspirations behind the artworks. This personal interaction enriches your experience, allowing you to appreciate the nuances of contemporary art in a more profound way.

Additionally, keep an eye out for art festivals and events that occur throughout the year in Parma. The city hosts several art fairs, exhibitions, and cultural festivals that celebrate local talent and creativity. These events often feature live performances, workshops, and interactive installations, providing a lively atmosphere for art enthusiasts and casual visitors alike. Participating in these community gatherings allows you to engage directly with the artistic community and witness the vibrancy of contemporary art in action.

In summary, engaging with local galleries in Parma is an enriching experience that reveals the city's contemporary artistic landscape. From established institutions to grassroots initiatives, these galleries showcase the diversity and creativity of modern artists. Whether you are exploring a temporary exhibition or attending an interactive event, your engagement with contemporary art in

Parma will enhance your understanding of the city's cultural identity and its ongoing evolution. Don't miss the chance to experience the pulse of Parma's art scene, as it offers a fresh perspective on a city steeped in history.

CHAPTER 4:

STROLL THROUGH CHARMING NEIGHBORHOODS

Wander The Picturesque Streets Of The Historic City Center

Wandering through the picturesque streets of Parma's historic city center is akin to stepping into a living postcard, where every corner reveals a new marvel waiting to be explored. The city's compact layout makes it ideal for leisurely strolls, allowing visitors to soak in the rich history and vibrant culture that define this charming Italian locale. The beauty of Parma lies not only in its stunning architecture but also in the stories that each street tells, making your walk an adventure filled with discoveries.

As you set foot in the historic center, the first thing that captures your attention is the intricate blend of Renaissance, Baroque, and Romanesque architecture that frames the streets. The iconic Piazza del Duomo is an excellent starting point for your exploration.

Dominated by the stunning Cathedral of Parma and the Baptistery, this square is a visual feast. The Cathedral, with its magnificent frescoed dome, invites you to gaze upward and appreciate the artistry of Correggio, while the Baptistery showcases exquisite pink Verona marble, featuring intricate sculptures and carvings. Take a moment to sit on a nearby bench and soak in the ambiance of the square, where locals and visitors alike gather to appreciate the beauty of their surroundings.

Continuing your journey, you'll find yourself on Strada della Repubblica, one of the main thoroughfares leading through the city center. This lively street is lined with shops, boutiques, and historic buildings, each with its own unique charm. As you wander, you might come across artisan shops offering handcrafted goods, from leather products to artisanal chocolates. Don't hesitate to step inside; many shopkeepers are eager to share their stories and the history behind their crafts, creating a warm and welcoming atmosphere.

For a taste of local life, head towards Via Farini, where you'll find an array of cafés and bakeries that entice you with the aroma of freshly baked pastries and rich espresso. Here, you can take a break and indulge in some of Parma's culinary delights. Treat yourself to a slice of torta fritta, a local specialty, or savor a cappuccino while observing the lively interactions of the locals. Many cafés offer outdoor seating, allowing you to bask in the sun and enjoy the vibrant street life that characterizes this historic area.

As you meander through the streets, keep an eye out for the colorful street art that adds a contemporary touch to the historic backdrop. Artists have embraced the walls of Parma as their canvas, infusing the city with creativity and a youthful spirit. Take the time to appreciate these artworks, which reflect the city's evolving identity while honoring its rich heritage.

Every street you explore tells a story, and you'll often stumble upon hidden gems such as charming alleyways and quaint squares. One such hidden square is Piazza della Pace, an intimate space where you can escape the hustle and bustle of the main streets. Here, you might find locals enjoying a leisurely afternoon, sipping wine, or playing chess under the shade of a tree. This square encapsulates the essence of Parma's community spirit, where time slows down, and connections are made.

In the evening, the city transforms as the sun sets, casting a warm glow over the historic center. The streets come alive with the sounds of laughter and conversation, as people gather for dinner in the many trattorias and osterias. Don't miss the chance to savor traditional dishes made with fresh, local ingredients, such as risotto alla Parmigiana or the famous Prosciutto di Parma. As you dine, you'll experience the warmth and hospitality that Parma is known for, with locals eager to share their love for their city and its culinary delights.

To truly immerse yourself in the local culture, consider joining a walking tour that focuses on the history and architecture of Parma. These tours are often led by knowledgeable guides who can provide insights into the city's past, including its role in the Italian Renaissance and its cultural significance. Many tours include stops at key landmarks and hidden corners that you might overlook on your own, ensuring you leave with a deeper appreciation for the city.

In summary, wandering the picturesque streets of Parma's historic city center is a delightful experience that allows you to engage with the city's rich history and vibrant culture. From the stunning architecture to the charming cafés and shops, every moment spent exploring this area reveals something new and enchanting. So lace up your walking shoes, take your time, and let the charm of Parma captivate you as you discover the heart of this beautiful Italian city.

Discover Hidden Squares Filled With Local Cafés And Shops

As you venture beyond the main thoroughfares of Parma, you'll find a treasure trove of hidden squares, each brimming with local charm and character. These lesser-known gems are the heart of the community, offering an authentic glimpse into everyday life in Parma. Exploring these squares allows you to escape the tourist crowds and immerse yourself in the warmth of local culture, where cafés and shops provide a perfect backdrop for relaxation and discovery.

One such hidden square is Piazza San Francesco, a quaint space that exudes a peaceful ambiance. Surrounded by historic buildings, this square features a lovely fountain at its center and is often filled with locals enjoying leisurely conversations. Here, you'll find cozy cafés that serve delightful pastries and excellent coffee. Consider taking a seat at one of the outdoor tables, where you can savor a slice of a traditional dessert, such as torta di riso, a rice cake that's both comforting and delicious. The café staff are usually friendly and welcoming, eager to recommend local specialties and share the history of their establishment.

As you explore further, don't miss Piazza della Libertà, a hidden gem that often goes unnoticed by tourists. This charming square is home to a few artisan shops and boutique stores where you can find unique handmade goods and local products. From handcrafted ceramics to traditional textiles, the offerings here reflect the rich craftsmanship that defines the region. Engaging with the shopkeepers can be a rewarding experience, as they often take pride in sharing their knowledge about the items they sell and the stories behind their creations.

For a truly authentic experience, visit the Mercato di Parma, held in a picturesque square every Saturday morning. This bustling market is a feast for the senses, with colorful stalls overflowing with fresh produce, artisanal cheeses, cured meats, and local delicacies. As you stroll through the market, the enticing aromas of freshly baked bread and rich cheeses fill the air, making it impossible to resist sampling the local fare. Engage with the vendors, who are more than happy to share their culinary expertise and recommendations for the best products. This is a fantastic opportunity to stock up on picnic supplies or bring a taste of Parma back home.

Another delightful square to discover is Piazza Ghiaia, a lively area where you can find a mix of shops and eateries. The square is known for its vibrant atmosphere, especially during the afternoons when locals gather to socialize. Here, you can enjoy a refreshing gelato from one of the nearby gelaterias, an essential treat on a warm day. As you savor your gelato, take a moment to appreciate the stunning architecture that surrounds the square, from the historic buildings to the charming fountains that add character to the scene.

As the sun begins to set, the squares of Parma take on a magical quality. The soft glow of streetlights illuminates the cobblestone paths, creating a romantic ambiance that beckons you to linger. Many cafés and restaurants offer outdoor seating, allowing you to enjoy a meal or drink al fresco while watching the world go by. The lively chatter and laughter of locals create a warm and inviting atmosphere, making it easy to feel like you're part of the community.

Engaging with the local culture in these hidden squares also provides an opportunity to witness traditional events and celebrations. Throughout the year, various festivals and fairs take place in these spaces, showcasing local music, art, and gastronomy. These events offer a chance to connect with the community and experience the vibrant spirit of Parma firsthand. Whether it's a food festival featuring regional delicacies or a music performance in the square, participating in these events will leave you with lasting memories of your time in the city.

In summary, discovering hidden squares filled with local cafés and shops is an enriching experience that reveals the authentic character of Parma. Each square offers a unique atmosphere, inviting you to relax, indulge in local delicacies, and engage with the friendly community. By taking the time to explore these lesser-known gems, you'll uncover the true essence of Parma, creating unforgettable memories that go beyond the typical tourist experience.

Experience The Warm Hospitality Of The People In Quaint Neighborhoods

One of the most enchanting aspects of Parma is the warm hospitality of its residents, which is especially evident in the city's quaint neighborhoods. As you wander through these charming areas, you'll encounter friendly locals eager to share their love for their city, making your visit feel like a genuine cultural exchange. The neighborhoods of Parma are filled with character, each with its unique personality and inviting atmosphere.

In neighborhoods like Oltretorrente, you'll find narrow, winding streets that lead you through a vibrant tapestry of colorful buildings adorned with blooming flowers. This area is known for its artistic vibe, with murals and street art that reflect the creativity of the local community. As you stroll along, you might come across artists at work, capturing the beauty of their surroundings on canvas or engaging in friendly conversations with passersby. The warmth of the locals adds to the neighborhood's charm, creating an environment that feels welcoming and inclusive.

Another delightful neighborhood to explore is Borgo della Salina, a picturesque area steeped in history. Here, you can admire the well-preserved architecture and quaint shops that line the streets. Take the time to visit local bakeries and specialty food stores, where the owners are often happy to share their family recipes and culinary secrets. Engaging with these local artisans allows you to appreciate the rich culinary traditions of Parma, and you may even find yourself inspired to try your hand at cooking some of the regional specialties.

Throughout the city, you'll encounter various community events that highlight the warmth and hospitality of the people. Many neighborhoods organize festivals celebrating local culture, music, and food, creating a lively atmosphere that invites participation. Joining in these events is a wonderful way to connect with the community and experience the joy of sharing in traditional customs. The smiles and laughter of the residents as they welcome visitors into their celebrations create a sense of belonging that is hard to find elsewhere.

When you visit local markets, you'll witness firsthand the generosity of the people of Parma. Vendors take pride in showcasing their produce, cheeses, and cured meats, often offering samples to passersby. This act of hospitality creates an inviting environment where you can learn about the local food culture and connect with the individuals who contribute to it. Engaging in conversations with these vendors can lead to recommendations for the best restaurants and hidden gems in the city, enhancing your overall experience.

Dining in the neighborhoods of Parma also reflects the city's hospitality. Family-owned trattorias and osterias welcome guests with open arms, treating you like part of their family. The owners often take the time to explain the menu, share stories about their culinary heritage, and ensure you feel at home during your meal. As you savor traditional dishes prepared with love and care, the genuine warmth of the staff creates an unforgettable dining experience that goes beyond the food itself.

The neighborhoods of Parma also foster a strong sense of community, with residents often gathering in parks and squares to socialize and unwind. You may find locals enjoying leisurely afternoons in the sun, playing games, or simply chatting with neighbors. These interactions showcase the close-knit nature of the community, where everyone is eager to connect and share a laugh. Embracing the local culture in this way allows you to experience Parma through the eyes of its residents, enriching your understanding of the city.

In summary, experiencing the warm hospitality of the people in Parma's quaint neighborhoods is a highlight of any visit to the city. The friendliness of the locals, combined with the charm of the neighborhoods, creates an inviting atmosphere that encourages exploration and connection. By engaging with the community and immersing yourself in the local culture, you'll leave Parma with cherished memories and a deeper appreciation for the city and its residents.

CHAPTER 5:

INDULGE IN PARMA'S SWEET TREATS

Satisfy Your Sweet Tooth With Local Delicacies Like Torta Fritta

When you think of Italian cuisine, images of pasta and pizza often come to mind. However, the desserts and sweets of Italy, particularly in regions like Emilia-Romagna, are equally enticing and worthy of exploration. In Parma, a city rich in culinary traditions, you can indulge your sweet tooth with local delicacies that reflect the area's unique flavors and techniques. Among these delights, torta fritta stands out as a beloved favorite that embodies the spirit of Italian hospitality and culinary creativity.

Torta fritta, also known as crescentine, is a traditional fried bread that holds a special place in the hearts of Parmigiani. It is often served warm, puffed up to a perfect golden-brown, and is typically accompanied by an array of local cured meats and cheeses. The beauty of torta fritta lies not only in its delightful taste but also in its versatility; it can be enjoyed as a savory snack or a sweet treat. When served as a sweet option, it may be sprinkled with sugar or served alongside fresh fruit preserves, making it a delightful addition to any meal or a satisfying dessert.

To truly appreciate torta fritta, consider visiting a local trattoria or osteria where this delicacy is a staple on the menu. Here, you'll have the chance to enjoy it in its most authentic form, often paired with local specialties like Prosciutto di Parma and Parmigiano-Reggiano cheese. The contrast of the crispy, airy torta with the richness of the meats and cheeses creates a harmonious flavor profile that exemplifies the essence of Emilia-Romagna's culinary tradition. Each bite is a celebration of local ingredients and age-old recipes, offering a glimpse into the heart of Parma's food culture.

Many local families have their own cherished recipes for torta fritta, passed down through generations. Some may use a hint of sparkling wine in the dough to add a unique flavor, while others rely on the quality of the flour and the precise frying technique to achieve the perfect texture. If you have the opportunity, participating in a cooking class can provide invaluable insight into this traditional dish. You'll learn not only how to prepare torta fritta but also about the cultural significance of this beloved bread and its role in the communal dining experience.

After savoring torta fritta, it's time to explore the sweeter side of Parma's dessert scene. The city is home to a variety of delectable pastries and confections, each showcasing the artistry of local bakers. Whether you have a penchant for creamy pastries or fruity desserts, Parma's bakeries offer something for everyone. One must-try pastry is the profiterole, a choux pastry filled with rich cream and often drizzled with chocolate. These light, airy delights are perfect for satisfying your cravings while exploring the city.

Additionally, crostata di frutta, a fresh fruit tart, is a popular choice among locals and visitors alike. Made with a buttery crust and filled with pastry cream, it is topped with an assortment of seasonal fruits that burst with flavor. A slice of crostata pairs beautifully with a cup of espresso, making it an ideal afternoon treat while taking a break from sightseeing.

When exploring bakeries in Parma, keep an eye out for panettoni and pandori, traditional Italian sweet breads often enjoyed during the holiday season. These rich, fluffy breads are infused with candied fruits and nuts, making them a festive indulgence that can be enjoyed year-round. Many local bakeries also produce artisanal versions of these treats, showcasing their craftsmanship and dedication to quality ingredients.

Visiting the historic city center of Parma, you'll find numerous bakeries and pastry shops offering a tantalizing array of sweets. From quaint storefronts with traditional wooden displays to modern establishments with innovative creations, each bakery reflects the local culture and passion for baked goods. Don't hesitate to strike up a conversation with the bakers; many are eager to share the stories behind their recipes and the secrets to their success.

In addition to traditional pastries, you'll discover a new wave of artisanal gelato shops that have gained popularity in recent years. Gelato is more than just ice cream; it is an art form that requires skill, precision, and a deep understanding of flavors and textures. Many gelato makers take pride in using high-quality, locally sourced ingredients, resulting in vibrant, intense flavors that capture the essence of the season.

Exploring gelato shops in Parma can be a delightful adventure, with countless flavors to choose from. Classic options like cioccolato (chocolate) and nocciola (hazelnut) are always crowd-pleasers, but don't shy away from trying more unique offerings like mascarpone with figs or pistachio with sea salt. The creamy texture and rich flavor of artisanal gelato are sure to impress even the most discerning dessert lover.

Learning about the art of making traditional Italian gelato can be an enriching experience.

Many gelaterias offer workshops and tastings, where you can gain insights into the process of crafting this beloved frozen treat. From selecting the finest ingredients to mastering the techniques of churning and freezing, these workshops provide a behind-the-scenes look at the dedication and craftsmanship that go into each batch of gelato.

As you savor torta fritta and indulge in the city's sweet offerings, take a moment to reflect on the importance of these culinary delights in Italian culture. Food in Italy is not just about sustenance; it is a celebration of life, family, and community. Sharing a meal, whether it be a hearty feast or a simple dessert, brings people together and creates lasting memories. In Parma, the combination of warm hospitality, rich culinary traditions, and delicious sweets creates an unforgettable experience that will linger in your heart long after you leave.

In conclusion, satisfying your sweet tooth in Parma is a journey filled with local delicacies like torta fritta, irresistible pastries, and the art of gelato making. Each bite tells a story, connecting you to the rich culinary heritage of this remarkable city. Whether you're enjoying torta fritta with friends, sampling pastries from a local bakery, or indulging in a scoop of gelato, the flavors of Parma will leave a lasting impression on your palate and your heart.

Learn About The Art Of Making Traditional Italian Gelato

The rich history and artistry of gelato making is a cherished tradition in Italy, and Parma is no exception. To truly appreciate this beloved frozen dessert, it is essential to understand the craft behind it, which is steeped in passion and expertise. From selecting the finest ingredients to mastering the perfect texture, the art of making traditional Italian gelato is a meticulous process that has been refined over centuries.

Gelato, which translates to "frozen" in Italian, is distinct from traditional ice cream in several ways. The key difference lies in its ingredients and preparation methods. While both gelato and ice cream are made from cream, sugar, and flavorings, gelato typically contains less cream and more milk, resulting in a lower fat content and a denser, silkier texture. Additionally, gelato is churned at a slower speed than ice cream, incorporating less air and creating a denser product that allows for a more intense flavor experience.

To gain a deeper understanding of the art of gelato making, consider participating in a workshop at a local gelateria. Many establishments in Parma offer hands-on classes that allow you to learn the basics of gelato preparation. These workshops often begin with an introduction to the essential ingredients, including high-quality milk, sugar, and natural flavorings. Local gelato makers emphasize the importance of using fresh, seasonal ingredients to create authentic flavors that capture the essence of the region.

During the workshop, you will learn how to combine the ingredients in precise measurements to achieve the perfect balance of sweetness and creaminess. The instructor will guide you through the process of heating the mixture, cooling it down, and allowing it to rest before churning. This resting phase is crucial, as it allows the flavors to meld together and enhances the overall taste of the gelato.

Once the base is ready, it is time to experiment with flavors. Traditional gelato flavors such as cioccolato and nocciola are often staples, but the real artistry comes in creating unique combinations that reflect the local culture. As you work with seasonal fruits, nuts, and other flavorings, you'll discover the joy of experimenting with textures and tastes. Learning to balance sweetness and acidity is an essential skill that gelato makers develop over time, allowing them to create flavors that are both harmonious and surprising.

After churning the gelato, it is important to understand the significance of the serving temperature. Gelato is typically served at a slightly warmer temperature than ice cream, which enhances its creamy texture and allows the flavors to shine through. This attention to detail is what sets traditional Italian gelato apart, and mastering this technique is crucial for any aspiring gelato maker.

Once you've completed the workshop, you will undoubtedly have a newfound appreciation for the craftsmanship that goes into each scoop of gelato. Many participants find joy in creating their own unique flavors and take pride in sharing their creations with friends and family. The experience of learning about gelato making not only enhances your culinary skills but also deepens your connection to Italian culture and traditions.

In addition to workshops, some gelaterias in Parma also host tasting events, where you can sample a variety of flavors while learning about the history of gelato. These tastings often include explanations of how different flavors are crafted and the stories behind each creation. Attending one of these events is a wonderful way to immerse yourself in the world of gelato, expanding your palate and discovering new favorites along the way.

As you explore the gelato scene in Parma, take the time to visit a few local gelaterias to experience the diversity of flavors available. Each gelateria has its unique spin on traditional recipes, often incorporating regional ingredients to create signature flavors. From tangy limone (lemon) to rich tiramisu, the choices are seemingly endless, and each scoop offers a taste of the artisan's passion and dedication.

Many gelaterias take pride in using sustainable practices, sourcing ingredients from local farms, and supporting the community. By choosing to enjoy gelato from these establishments, you contribute to the local economy and help preserve the culinary traditions that make Parma a delightful destination for food lovers.

In conclusion, learning about the art of making traditional Italian gelato in Parma is an enriching experience that deepens your appreciation for this beloved treat. From the meticulous selection of ingredients to the delicate process of churning and serving, gelato making embodies the passion and creativity of Italian cuisine. Whether you participate in a workshop, attend a tasting event, or simply enjoy a scoop from a local gelateria, the flavors of Parma's gelato scene are sure to leave a lasting impression.

Visit Bakeries Known For Their Irresistible Pastries And Cakes

Exploring the bakeries of Parma is a delightful adventure filled with irresistible pastries and cakes that showcase the city's rich culinary heritage. From traditional treats to innovative creations, Parma's bakeries offer a tempting array of sweets that cater to every palate. Each bakery reflects the artistry and craftsmanship of its bakers, making them a must-visit for anyone with a sweet tooth.

As you stroll through the historic streets of Parma, the aroma of freshly baked goods wafts through the air, drawing you into quaint bakeries filled with delicious pastries. One of the standout items to try is brioche, a sweet, soft bread often enjoyed for breakfast. The flaky layers of a well-made brioche are perfect when paired with a cup of coffee or a creamy hot chocolate. Many bakeries offer variations of brioche, filled with cream, fruit preserves, or chocolate, elevating this simple treat to new heights.

Another beloved pastry to sample is the torta della nonna, a classic Tuscan dessert that has found a special place in the hearts of Parmigiani. This custard tart is made with a buttery pastry crust and filled with rich, creamy custard, then topped with pine nuts and a dusting of powdered sugar. Each bite of torta della nonna is a comforting experience, reminiscent of homemade desserts enjoyed in the warmth of a grandmother's kitchen.

As you explore the bakeries, don't miss out on cannoncini, a delectable pastry resembling a cream horn. These flaky pastries are filled with rich pastry cream and often topped with a dusting of powdered sugar. The contrast between the crispy exterior and the smooth, creamy filling makes cannoncini an indulgent treat that pairs wonderfully with an afternoon coffee or tea.

For those with a penchant for chocolate, look for torta al cioccolato, a rich chocolate cake that is a highlight in many local bakeries. This decadent dessert is made with high-quality chocolate and is often served with a dollop of fresh whipped cream or a scoop of gelato.

The intense chocolate flavor combined with the light texture of the cake creates a heavenly experience for chocolate lovers.

Exploring Parma's bakeries also offers an opportunity to discover seasonal specialties that celebrate local ingredients. During the summer months, you may find pastries filled with fresh fruits, while winter brings rich, spiced treats that warm the soul. By visiting different bakeries throughout the year, you can experience the changing flavors and culinary innovations that reflect the seasons and the local culture.

Many bakeries in Parma embrace the farm-to-table philosophy, sourcing ingredients from local producers to create high-quality pastries and cakes. By supporting these bakeries, you contribute to the local economy while enjoying some of the finest sweets the region has to offer. Engaging with the bakers and learning about their sourcing practices can also deepen your appreciation for the craft behind each creation.

As you indulge in the sweet offerings of Parma, consider taking a bakery tour that showcases the city's finest establishments. These tours often include tastings of various pastries and cakes, allowing you to sample a range of flavors and textures while learning about the history and techniques behind each dessert. A bakery tour is an excellent way to immerse yourself in Parma's culinary scene and discover hidden gems that you may not find on your own.

In conclusion, visiting bakeries known for their irresistible pastries and cakes in Parma is a delightful experience for anyone with a sweet tooth. From classic treats like brioche and torta della nonna to innovative creations that highlight seasonal ingredients, the city's bakeries are a treasure trove of flavors and textures. As you explore the sweet side of Parma, each bite will take you on a culinary journey that reflects the rich traditions and artistry of Italian baking.

CHAPTER 6:

RELAX IN BEAUTIFUL PARKS AND GARDENS

Enjoy A Leisurely Afternoon In The Parco Ducale

Enjoying a leisurely afternoon in Parma offers a unique opportunity to immerse yourself in the beauty of its parks and gardens. Among the highlights are the Parco Ducale and Giardino della Ghiara, each providing a distinct experience that captures the essence of Italian leisure. The lush greenery, tranquil atmosphere, and range of outdoor activities make these spaces perfect for both relaxation and recreation.

The Parco Ducale, or Duke's Park, is one of the most celebrated green spaces in Parma. Originally designed in the 16th century for the Duke of Parma, this historic park spans around 60 acres, boasting a stunning array of trees, flowers, and scenic pathways. As you stroll through the park, you'll be greeted by the sight of majestic sycamores, lush lawns, and vibrant flowerbeds that change with the seasons, creating a picturesque landscape throughout the year. The gentle sounds of chirping birds and rustling leaves enhance the serene ambiance, making it an ideal spot to unwind and enjoy nature.

One of the park's most striking features is the central pond, where swans glide gracefully across the water. This serene setting is perfect for quiet contemplation, reading a book, or simply enjoying the beauty around you. The park is equipped with benches strategically placed along pathways, allowing visitors to sit and soak in the tranquility or engage in conversations with friends or loved ones. Whether you choose to people-watch or admire the view, the peaceful surroundings provide a welcome escape from the hustle and bustle of city life.

For those looking to engage in outdoor activities, the Parco Ducale offers plenty of options. The expansive lawns provide ample space for picnicking, playing frisbee, or even practicing yoga under the open sky. Many locals flock to the park to engage in jogging or leisurely walks, especially in the early morning or late afternoon when the temperatures are cooler and the light casts a warm glow over the landscape. If you're traveling with children, they'll delight in the playground area designed for younger visitors, making it a family-friendly destination.

As you explore the Parco Ducale, take a moment to appreciate its historical significance. The park is home to several elegant statues and fountains that reflect Parma's artistic heritage. The fountain of the Goddess Diana, located at the park's entrance, is a stunning example of Baroque sculpture and serves as a fitting welcome to visitors. The surrounding gardens and pathways lead you past various monuments and artistic installations, creating an outdoor gallery that highlights the city's rich cultural history.

Discover The Lush Greenery And Tranquil Atmosphere Of Giardino Della Ghiara

After spending some time in the Parco Ducale, consider venturing to the nearby Giardino della Ghiara. This hidden gem is situated next to the church of San Giovanni Evangelista and offers a more intimate garden experience. The Giardino della Ghiara is smaller in size compared to Parco Ducale but is no less enchanting. As you enter the garden, you'll immediately notice the well-maintained flower beds, manicured hedges, and the peaceful ambiance that envelops the space. The garden is often less crowded, allowing visitors to enjoy a more private atmosphere, making it a perfect spot for reflection or a quiet escape.

In Giardino della Ghiara, you'll find an impressive collection of plants and flowers, many of which are native to the region. The vibrant blooms create a stunning visual display that changes throughout the seasons. Spring brings a burst of color as tulips and daffodils emerge from the ground, while summer showcases an array of roses in full bloom. Autumn's palette transforms the garden into a tapestry of reds, oranges, and yellows, making each visit a unique experience.

The garden's layout encourages leisurely strolls along winding paths that lead you to hidden corners and cozy seating areas. These secluded spots are perfect for finding a quiet bench to sit and enjoy the beauty of nature. The gentle sound of water from the small fountain adds to the peaceful ambiance, creating a serene backdrop for relaxation. As you sit and take in your surroundings, you might spot a few butterflies fluttering among the flowers or hear the distant laughter of children playing nearby.

For those who enjoy photography, Giardino della Ghiara presents countless opportunities to capture the beauty of the flora and the charm of the garden. The interplay of light and shadow, particularly during the golden hours of sunrise and sunset, creates a magical atmosphere. Whether you're an amateur or a professional photographer, you'll find plenty of inspiring subjects, from close-ups of delicate petals to wide shots of the garden's serene landscape.

Another unique aspect of Giardino della Ghiara is its cultural significance. The garden is often used for art exhibitions and community events, showcasing the work of local artists and craftsmen. Participating in these events provides an opportunity to engage with the local community and gain insight into the cultural fabric of Parma. You may find yourself wandering through an exhibition of contemporary art installations or enjoying a live music performance under the shade of the trees.

Engage In Outdoor Activities While Soaking Up The Italian Sun

Engaging in outdoor activities while soaking up the Italian sun is an integral part of the Parma experience. Both the Parco Ducale and Giardino della Ghiara encourage visitors to embrace the beauty of nature and lead an active lifestyle. The mild Mediterranean climate makes outdoor exploration enjoyable year-round, with warm summers perfect for picnics and cool autumns ideal for leisurely walks.

Consider bringing along a blanket and a delicious picnic spread, complete with local cheeses, cured meats, fresh fruits, and a bottle of Italian wine. Finding a shady spot under a tree in Parco Ducale allows you to savor your meal while surrounded by nature. As you indulge in the flavors of Parma, the delightful setting elevates the experience, making it even more memorable.

If you prefer a more organized activity, look for outdoor fitness classes offered in Parco Ducale. Many local instructors host yoga, Pilates, or tai chi sessions, allowing you to connect with nature while engaging in physical wellness. Joining a class is an excellent way to meet fellow travelers or locals who share your interest in fitness and well-being.

Cycling is another fantastic way to explore these parks and their surroundings. Renting a bike allows you to cover more ground while enjoying the scenic views at your own pace. Cycling paths weave through the Parco Ducale, making it easy to enjoy a leisurely ride while taking in the fresh air and beautiful scenery. As you pedal along, you may discover hidden nooks and crannies of the park that you might otherwise miss.

As your afternoon unfolds, consider engaging in a game of petanque, a traditional French game similar to boules, which has gained popularity in Italy. Many parks, including the Parco Ducale, have designated areas for this outdoor game. Playing petanque is a great way to socialize with friends or meet new people, as locals often invite newcomers to join in the fun. The combination of friendly competition and laughter creates an inviting atmosphere that embodies the essence of Italian leisure.

As the day draws to a close, take a moment to reflect on your experiences in these beautiful parks. The gentle setting sun casts a warm golden hue over the landscape, creating a magical ambiance that invites you to linger a little longer. The Parco Ducale and Giardino della Ghiara serve as reminders of the importance of leisure and connection with nature in our busy lives.

In conclusion, spending a leisurely afternoon in the Parco Ducale and Giardino della Ghiara is a delightful way to experience the natural beauty and cultural richness of Parma. From the expansive lawns and historical monuments of Parco Ducale to the intimate gardens and vibrant flowers of Giardino della Ghiara, each space offers a unique opportunity for relaxation and outdoor activities. Whether you're enjoying a picnic, engaging in outdoor sports, or simply soaking up the Italian sun, these parks invite you to slow down and appreciate the beauty that surrounds you. Embrace the tranquility and charm of Parma's green spaces, and let them enrich your experience in this enchanting Italian city.

CHAPTER 7:

ATTEND LOCAL FESTIVALS AND EVENTS

Experience The Excitement Of The Annual Fiera Di San Giovanni

The Fiera di San Giovanni is an exciting annual event that transforms the city of Parma into a bustling hub of culture, tradition, and community spirit. This vibrant fair is held in mid-June to honor Saint John the Baptist, the city's patron saint, and it attracts locals and tourists alike. The Fiera di San Giovanni is not just a festival; it's an integral part of Parma's cultural identity, showcasing the rich traditions that define this charming city.

As the fair kicks off, the streets of Parma come alive with an array of colorful stalls and vendors selling everything from handcrafted goods to delicious local delicacies. The excitement is palpable as you walk through the bustling market, where the sounds of laughter, music, and the sizzling of street food fill the air. The event typically spans several days, providing ample opportunity to explore the festivities, engage with local artisans, and sample the culinary delights that make Parma famous.

Among the highlights of the Fiera di San Giovanni are the traditional food stalls that offer a wide selection of local specialties. This is the perfect chance to savor authentic Parmigiano Reggiano cheese, freshly baked torta fritta, and various cured meats. Many vendors provide tastings, allowing you to indulge in the rich flavors that characterize Parma's culinary scene. As you enjoy these delights, you'll gain insight into the region's gastronomic heritage and the artisanal methods that have been passed down through generations.

Cultural performances are another essential component of the Fiera di San Giovanni. Various groups take to the stage to showcase traditional music, dance, and theater, providing entertainment that captivates audiences of all ages. You might witness a lively folk dance performance, where colorful costumes swirl in rhythm to the sounds of traditional instruments, or hear a local choir serenading visitors with beautiful melodies. These performances are not only entertaining but also serve to educate attendees about Parma's history and cultural diversity.

Throughout the fair, there are also workshops and demonstrations where you can learn more about local crafts. Artisans often set up booths to demonstrate their skills, whether it's pottery, weaving, or glassblowing. Participating in these workshops is a fantastic way to immerse yourself in the local culture and even take home a handmade souvenir as a reminder of your experience. These interactive sessions foster a sense of community and allow visitors to connect with the passionate craftsmen behind the creations.

For families, the Fiera di San Giovanni is a fantastic outing. Children can enjoy various activities, including face painting, puppet shows, and rides that fill the fairgrounds with laughter and joy. The festival atmosphere creates a safe and welcoming environment for families, encouraging them to explore and engage in the festivities together. The combination of cultural events, culinary delights, and family-friendly activities ensures that there's something for everyone at the fair.

As the sun sets, the Fiera di San Giovanni transforms into a magical experience. The twinkling lights strung above the stalls create a warm and inviting atmosphere, while the sounds of music and laughter fill the night air. Many visitors enjoy strolling hand-in-hand through the fair, soaking in the ambiance and relishing the memories created during the day. If you're lucky, you might even catch a fireworks display that lights up the night sky, providing a spectacular finale to the festival.

Join The Celebrations Of The Festival Of Prosciutto Di Parma

The Festival of Prosciutto di Parma is another highlight of Parma's cultural calendar, celebrating one of the region's most iconic products. This festival typically takes place in September and draws food enthusiasts from around the world eager to experience the rich flavors and culinary heritage of Prosciutto di Parma. The festival serves as a tribute to the craftsmanship and tradition that goes into producing this world-renowned delicacy, making it a must-visit event for any food lover.

At the heart of the festival is the opportunity to taste various types of Prosciutto di Parma, each with its unique flavor profile and texture. Local producers showcase their best hams, and visitors are invited to sample these artisanal products. Many tastings are guided by knowledgeable experts who can explain the differences between the various aging processes and production methods. You'll learn how the hams are carefully crafted, cured, and aged, resulting in the distinctive sweetness and tenderness that Prosciutto di Parma is famous for.

Throughout the festival, there are numerous culinary demonstrations and workshops focused on the versatility of Prosciutto di Parma in Italian cuisine. Renowned chefs often participate, sharing their expertise and offering innovative recipes that incorporate the ham in creative ways. These demonstrations not only highlight the culinary possibilities of Prosciutto di Parma but also showcase the region's broader gastronomic culture. Attendees can learn how to pair the ham with different cheeses, fruits, and wines, enhancing their culinary knowledge and experience.

In addition to food, the Festival of Prosciutto di Parma features live music, dance performances, and cultural activities that highlight the rich heritage of the region. Local musicians perform traditional tunes, filling the air with lively melodies that invite attendees to dance and celebrate. The festival atmosphere is infectious, creating a sense of camaraderie among visitors as they share their love for food, music, and culture. Artisans also set up booths to sell local crafts, providing an opportunity to take home a piece of Parma's vibrant culture.

One of the festival's most popular events is the Prosciutto di Parma Parade, where local producers proudly showcase their best hams. This colorful procession is a sight to behold, with participants dressed in traditional attire and carrying their prized hams through the streets of Parma. The parade culminates in a festive gathering where visitors can cheer on their favorite producers and learn more about the history of Prosciutto di Parma. This lively celebration reinforces the community spirit that characterizes the festival and emphasizes the importance of local craftsmanship.

For those looking to enhance their festival experience, consider participating in guided tours that explore the local food scene and historical sites related to Prosciutto di Parma. These tours often include visits to production facilities, allowing you to see firsthand how the ham is made and meet the artisans behind the process. Many tours also incorporate tastings at local restaurants that specialize in Prosciutto di Parma dishes, ensuring a comprehensive culinary adventure.

The Festival of Prosciutto di Parma is not only a celebration of food but also an opportunity to connect with the local community and learn about the traditions that define this beautiful region. Whether you're a seasoned foodie or simply curious about Italian cuisine, the festival promises an unforgettable experience filled with flavors, culture, and camaraderie.

Discover Cultural Events That Showcase Parma's Rich Heritage

Beyond the Fiera di San Giovanni and the Festival of Prosciutto di Parma, Parma boasts a diverse array of cultural events that highlight its rich heritage throughout the year. From art exhibitions and music festivals to historical reenactments and traditional fairs, the city offers a vibrant cultural scene that reflects its history and artistic contributions. Engaging in these events provides an authentic glimpse into Parma's past and present, fostering a deeper appreciation for its cultural identity.

One of the notable events in Parma's cultural calendar is the Parma Jazz Frontiere Festival, a celebration of jazz music that attracts international talent and local musicians. Held in various venues across the city, the festival showcases a range of performances, from traditional jazz to contemporary fusion. The festival's intimate settings create a unique atmosphere, allowing audiences to connect with the artists and experience the music up close. Attending the Parma Jazz Frontiere Festival is an excellent way to explore the city's cultural diversity and enjoy live performances that resonate with the spirit of creativity.

Art enthusiasts will appreciate the numerous exhibitions held throughout the year at local galleries and museums, including the Galleria Nazionale and the Museo di Glauco Lombardi. These institutions often host temporary exhibitions that feature works by both established and emerging artists, providing a platform for creativity and innovation. The exhibitions frequently explore themes relevant to contemporary society while also honoring the artistic heritage of Parma. Visitors can immerse themselves in the world of art, discovering the stories behind the works and the artists who created them.

Additionally, historical reenactments take place in various locations throughout Parma, allowing visitors to step back in time and experience life as it was in different eras.

These events often include costumed actors, traditional crafts, and interactive activities, creating an engaging experience for all ages. Whether it's a medieval fair or a Renaissance celebration, participating in these reenactments fosters a sense of connection to Parma's rich history and provides a fun and educational outing for families and visitors.

Local theaters also contribute to the cultural landscape of Parma, hosting performances that range from classic plays to contemporary productions. The Teatro Regio di Parma, one of Italy's premier opera houses, is renowned for its exceptional performances and exquisite architecture. Attending an opera or concert at the Teatro Regio is a quintessential Parma experience, offering a glimpse into the city's artistic heritage. The theater often features both local and international talent, ensuring a diverse program that appeals to a wide audience.

In addition to these cultural events, Parma hosts various food and wine festivals throughout the year that celebrate the region's gastronomic heritage. These events allow visitors to sample local delicacies, attend cooking classes, and engage with food producers who are passionate about their craft. Events like the Sagra del Culatello highlight traditional Italian cured meats, while the Festa della Gastronomia showcases the rich flavors of Parma's culinary landscape. These festivals create a vibrant atmosphere, inviting visitors to celebrate the flavors that define Parma while connecting with local producers and chefs.

As you explore Parma, take the time to seek out these cultural events, as they offer valuable insights into the city's history and traditions. Engaging with the local community through festivals, performances, and exhibitions allows you to experience the warmth and hospitality that define Parma. Whether you're indulging in culinary delights, immersing yourself in the arts, or participating in historical reenactments, you'll leave with lasting memories and a deeper appreciation for this beautiful Italian city.

In conclusion, the cultural events in Parma, including the Fiera di San Giovanni, the

Festival of Prosciutto di Parma, and various artistic celebrations, create a dynamic tapestry of experiences that reflect the city's rich heritage. From culinary delights to vibrant performances, each event invites visitors to immerse themselves in the local culture and discover the unique flavors and traditions that make Parma a captivating destination. Whether you're a local or a traveler, joining these celebrations promises to enrich your understanding of Parma and leave you with cherished memories.

CHAPTER 8:

EXPLORE THE SURROUNDING COUNTRYSIDE

Take A Scenic Drive Through The Stunning Emilia-Romagna Region

Emilia-Romagna, often referred to as the gastronomic heart of Italy, is a region that offers breathtaking landscapes, rich history, and unparalleled culinary experiences. A scenic drive through this region reveals rolling hills, lush vineyards, and charming villages, all set against the backdrop of the Apennine Mountains. Whether you're an avid traveler or simply looking for a relaxing getaway, exploring Emilia-Romagna by car provides a unique perspective on its stunning beauty and vibrant culture.

As you embark on your journey, consider starting in Bologna, the region's capital and a hub of culture and cuisine. The city is renowned for its medieval architecture and vibrant atmosphere, making it the perfect launch point for your scenic adventure. Before you hit the road, take a moment to explore Bologna's historic center, where you can visit iconic sites such as the Two Towers, the Basilica di San Petronio, and the Archiginnasio, the oldest university in the world. Don't forget to indulge in some local specialties like tortellini and ragù alla bolognese, which are emblematic of the region's culinary prowess.

Once you're ready to hit the road, head south towards Modena, a city famous for its balsamic vinegar and vibrant food scene. The drive from Bologna to Modena takes you through picturesque countryside dotted with vineyards and orchards. As you navigate the winding roads, take in the stunning vistas that unfold before you. You might spot rows of grapevines climbing the hillsides, and the sweet scent of fruit trees fills the air, setting the stage for your culinary exploration.

In Modena, a visit to a traditional acetaia (balsamic vinegar producer) is a must. Many local producers offer tours that take you through the process of creating authentic Modena balsamic vinegar, from grape selection to the aging process. You'll learn about the meticulous craftsmanship that goes into producing this prized condiment, which has been a staple of Italian cuisine for centuries. Tasting the rich, complex flavors of aged balsamic vinegar drizzled over cheese or strawberries is an unforgettable experience that showcases the region's culinary artistry.

From Modena, continue your journey to the town of Reggio Emilia, known for its vibrant culinary scene and beautiful squares. As you drive through the countryside, you'll notice small villages that seem to emerge from the landscape, each with its own charm and character. Stop in one of these villages to explore the local markets, where you can sample fresh produce, cheese, and cured meats. Engaging with the locals provides a glimpse into the rich traditions and customs that define life in Emilia-Romagna.

After soaking in the local culture, make your way towards Parma, another gem of the Emilia-Romagna region. Known for its cheese and ham, Parma offers a unique blend of culinary delights and historical attractions. A visit to a Parmigiano-Reggiano cheese factory is essential. Here, you'll witness the cheese-making process firsthand and learn about the stringent regulations that ensure the quality of this world-renowned cheese. Sampling freshly grated Parmigiano-Reggiano paired with local wines is a delicious way to appreciate the region's culinary heritage.

As you continue your drive, take the scenic route through the hills of the Apennines. The landscape becomes more rugged and dramatic, with sweeping views of valleys and forests. This area is perfect for outdoor enthusiasts, with numerous hiking trails and opportunities for birdwatching. The tranquility of the countryside provides a refreshing escape from the hustle and bustle of city life. Consider stopping at a roadside agriturismo, where you can savor a traditional meal made from locally sourced ingredients while enjoying the peaceful surroundings.

The drive then leads you to the charming town of Castell'Arquato, where medieval architecture reigns supreme. The well-preserved castle and historic buildings make this village a picturesque stop along your journey. Wander the cobblestone streets, exploring the quaint shops and cafes that offer regional specialties. A leisurely stroll through Castell'Arquato's historic center provides an opportunity to appreciate the craftsmanship and artistry that define the region's architectural heritage.

As your journey continues, head towards the wine-producing region of Emilia-Romagna. The area is renowned for its exceptional wines, particularly Lambrusco, a sparkling red wine that pairs beautifully with the region's rich cuisine. Many vineyards in the area welcome visitors for tastings and tours, offering a chance to learn about the winemaking process and sample a variety of wines. As you sip on a glass of Lambrusco, take in the stunning views of the vineyards stretching across the rolling hills, with the sun setting in the distance, casting a golden hue over the landscape.

Visit Vineyards Producing World-Renowned Wines Like Lambrusco

Lambrusco is a wine that truly embodies the spirit of Emilia-Romagna. Unlike the image of cheap, sugary wines that it sometimes carries, Lambrusco is a versatile and food-friendly wine that ranges from dry to sweet, offering a delightful balance of acidity and fruitiness. The grape variety itself has a long history in the region, and it thrives in the fertile soil and temperate climate, producing wines that reflect the local terroir.

Visiting a Lambrusco vineyard is an essential part of your Emilia-Romagna experience. Many vineyards offer guided tours that take you through the grape-growing process, from vine to bottle. You'll learn about the various types of Lambrusco grapes, including Lambrusco di Sorbara, Lambrusco Grasparossa, and Lambrusco Salamino, each offering unique flavor profiles and characteristics. The passionate vintners often share stories about their family traditions and the history of winemaking in the region, providing a personal touch to your visit.

During your vineyard tour, be sure to participate in a tasting session. Many vineyards provide a selection of their wines, often paired with local cheeses and cured meats. This gastronomic experience allows you to discover how the bright acidity of Lambrusco complements the savory flavors of local cuisine. As you savor each sip, the stunning views of the vineyards and surrounding hills enhance the experience, creating a picturesque setting for your wine tasting.

One highly recommended vineyard to visit is Cleto Chiarli, a historic winery in the heart of the Lambrusco production area. Founded in 1860, Cleto Chiarli has a rich legacy of winemaking and is known for its high-quality Lambrusco. During your visit, you can explore the vineyards, learn about their sustainable practices, and taste a selection of their wines, including their award-winning Grasparossa. The knowledgeable staff will guide you through the tasting, sharing insights into the unique characteristics of each wine and how they reflect the terroir of Emilia-Romagna.

Another notable vineyard is Medici Ermete, a family-run winery that produces exceptional Lambrusco wines using traditional methods. The winery offers tours that highlight their commitment to quality and sustainability, along with tastings of their various Lambrusco labels. Be sure to try their Reggiano Lambrusco, which showcases the bold, fruity flavors characteristic of the region.

After a day of wine tasting, consider exploring nearby towns such as Sorbara or Castelvetro di Modena. Both towns offer charming streets to wander and local eateries where you can enjoy traditional Emilia-Romagna dishes paired with the wines you've just tasted. The combination of local cuisine and Lambrusco creates a delightful dining experience that highlights the region's culinary heritage.

Experience The Charm Of Small Villages That Dot The Countryside

As you continue your scenic drive through Emilia-Romagna, the charm of its small villages is sure to captivate you. Each village has its own unique character, offering a glimpse into the region's history and culture. From quaint streets lined with colorful houses to stunning churches and local markets, these villages provide a refreshing contrast to the larger cities and allow you to experience the slower pace of rural life.

One such village is Dozza, known for its artistic heritage and vibrant murals. Nestled atop a hill, Dozza is famous for its Biennale del Muro Dipinto (Biennial of Painted Walls), where artists from around the world create stunning murals that adorn the village's buildings. Strolling through the narrow streets, you'll be amazed by the creativity and talent displayed in each mural. The village also boasts a medieval fortress, the Rocca di Dozza, which offers panoramic views of the surrounding countryside. Be sure to visit the local enoteca, where you can sample regional wines and purchase a bottle to take home.

Another charming stop is Brisighella, a picturesque village that boasts a rich history dating back to the Middle Ages. The village is known for its three distinctive hills, each topped with a historical structure: the Rocca Manfrediana, a fortress; the Monticino, a sanctuary; and the Torre dell'Orologio, a clock tower. Climbing to the top of these hills rewards you with stunning views of the surrounding hills and valleys. The winding streets of Brisighella are filled with artisan shops, cafes, and local restaurants, where you can enjoy traditional dishes made with locally sourced ingredients.

As you drive through Emilia-Romagna, you'll encounter other charming villages like Sant'Agata Bolognese, famous for being the home of Lamborghini, and the enchanting village of Vignola, known for its cherry blossoms and stunning castle. Each village you visit offers opportunities to meet locals, learn about their customs, and savor authentic regional cuisine.

The hospitality of the people in these small villages is one of the region's most endearing qualities. Locals are often eager to share their stories and recommend their favorite spots, whether it's a hidden trattoria serving homemade pasta or a quaint café with the best gelato in town. Engaging with the community enriches your experience and creates lasting memories of your journey through Emilia-Romagna.

As the sun sets, the golden light casts a warm glow over the villages, creating a magical ambiance that invites you to linger. Consider staying overnight in one of these charming towns, where cozy accommodations allow you to relax and fully immerse yourself in the local culture. Waking up to the sounds of the countryside and enjoying a traditional Italian breakfast at a local café is a delightful way to start your day.

Emilia-Romagna is a region that invites exploration, from its stunning landscapes and world-renowned wines to its charming villages and warm hospitality. A scenic drive through this beautiful region promises to leave you with unforgettable memories, delicious culinary experiences, and a deeper appreciation for the rich heritage that defines Emilia-Romagna.

CHAPTER 9:

DISCOVER THE REGION'S RICH HISTORY

Learn About Parma's Role In The Renaissance Period

Parma, a city renowned for its art, culture, and cuisine, played a significant role during the Renaissance period, a time of profound change and development in Italy. Nestled in the Emilia-Romagna region, Parma was not only an essential political and economic center but also a hub of artistic and intellectual activity. Understanding Parma's influence during the Renaissance provides insight into its cultural legacy that continues to thrive today.

The Renaissance in Parma is often associated with the rise of influential families, particularly the Farnese, who played a crucial role in shaping the city's cultural landscape. Under the Farnese dukes, especially Alessandro Farnese and his grandson, Ranuccio I Farnese, Parma became a center for the arts and scholarship. They patronized numerous artists, architects, and scholars, fostering an environment where creativity could flourish. The family's support led to the construction of magnificent palaces, churches, and public buildings that showcased the grandeur of Renaissance architecture.

One of the most significant landmarks from this era is the Palazzo della Pilotta, a massive complex built by the Farnese family in the 16th century. This architectural masterpiece served multiple purposes, housing a theater, art galleries, and the Ducal Palace. The Pilotta exemplifies the grandeur of Renaissance architecture, with its elegant courtyards and impressive facades. Within its walls, you can find the Teatro Farnese, one of the oldest wooden theaters in the world, designed by Giovanni Battista Aleotti. This theater remains a testament to the artistic achievements of the time, where performances captivated audiences with their elaborate sets and costumes.

Parma's role in the Renaissance also extends to the realm of painting. The city was home to several prominent artists, including Correggio, who became known for his innovative use of light and perspective. His works, such as the frescoes in the Cathedral of Parma and the Church of San Giovanni Evangelista, showcase the emotional depth and dynamic composition characteristic of the Renaissance style. Visitors can marvel at the stunning ceiling frescoes in the Cathedral, which depict scenes from the life of Christ and the Virgin Mary, demonstrating Correggio's mastery of illusion and spatial depth.

In addition to Correggio, Parmigianino emerged as another influential painter during the Renaissance. His unique style, characterized by elongated forms and a focus on beauty, set him apart from his contemporaries. Parmigianino's work can be seen in various locations throughout Parma, including the Church of Santa Maria della Steccata, where his famous painting "Madonna with the Long Neck" can be found. This masterpiece exemplifies his innovative approach and has solidified his place in art history.

Visit Museums That House Artifacts From Various Historical Eras

Parma's rich history is preserved in its numerous museums, each offering a glimpse into different eras and aspects of the city's heritage. One of the most prominent is the Galleria Nazionale di Parma, located within the Palazzo della Pilotta. This art gallery houses an extensive collection of Renaissance paintings, sculptures, and decorative arts. Notable works include pieces by Correggio, Parmigianino, and other significant artists of the period. The Galleria's layout allows visitors to appreciate the evolution of art in Parma, with a dedicated section for Baroque and 19th-century works as well.

The museum also features a remarkable collection of Renaissance tapestries and decorative arts, showcasing the intricate craftsmanship that flourished during this time. The opportunity to view these artifacts in their historical context enhances the visitor's understanding of the cultural climate of the Renaissance, illustrating how art and craftsmanship intertwined to reflect the values and aesthetics of the period.

Another important museum is the Museo Archeologico Nazionale di Parma, which offers insights into the city's ancient past. This museum houses artifacts from the Roman era, including statues, pottery, and inscriptions that highlight Parma's significance during Roman times. Visitors can explore exhibits that chronicle the city's development from its origins to the Renaissance, providing a comprehensive understanding of its historical evolution.

The Museo di Storia Naturale di Parma is also worth a visit, showcasing the city's relationship with the natural world. This museum features exhibits on local flora and fauna, geology, and paleontology, allowing visitors to appreciate the region's natural history. By exploring these various museums, visitors can gain a deeper appreciation for Parma's cultural heritage and its connections to broader historical narratives.

In addition to traditional museums, Parma hosts several temporary exhibitions and cultural events that highlight contemporary interpretations of its historical legacy. Art fairs, workshops, and lectures often take place in the city, inviting both locals and visitors to engage with the past while fostering a dialogue about its relevance in today's world. These events create a dynamic cultural atmosphere that encourages exploration and appreciation of Parma's diverse heritage.

Explore The Connections Between Parma And Notable Historical Figures

Parma's historical significance is intertwined with various notable figures who have shaped the city's cultural and political landscape. One of the most celebrated personalities associated with Parma is Giuseppe Verdi, one of the most influential composers in the history of opera. Born in a nearby village, Verdi's connection to Parma is profound, as he studied and performed in the city's theaters. The Teatro Regio di Parma, a prominent opera house, is a testament to his legacy and remains a venue for performances of his works.

Verdi's influence on Parma extends beyond music; he became a symbol of Italian unification during the 19th century. His operas, often centered on themes of love, sacrifice, and patriotism, resonated deeply with the Italian populace. Visitors to Parma can explore the Verdi Museum, located in his birthplace of Roncole Verdi, where artifacts and memorabilia highlight his life and contributions to music. This museum offers a unique insight into the artistic environment that nurtured Verdi's talent and showcases his enduring impact on Italian culture.

Another prominent figure connected to Parma is the philosopher and writer Giambattista Vico, known for his influential ideas on history and culture. Vico spent time in Parma during the late 17th century, and his works on the philosophy of history have left a lasting legacy. Exploring Vico's writings provides an understanding of how Parma contributed to intellectual discourse during the Renaissance and beyond.

In addition to these figures, Parma was home to various scholars, poets, and artists who contributed to the city's rich cultural tapestry. The legacy of the Farnese family, who played a pivotal role in the city's development, is also essential to understanding Parma's historical significance. Their patronage of artists and intellectuals created a vibrant cultural environment that attracted talent from across Italy and beyond.

Today, Parma continues to celebrate its historical connections through cultural events and festivals that pay homage to its rich heritage. The annual Verdi Festival, held in honor of the composer, draws music lovers from around the world, showcasing opera performances in the stunning Teatro Regio. This festival not only highlights Verdi's contributions to music but also reinforces Parma's reputation as a cultural hub.

In summary, Parma's role in the Renaissance period, its wealth of museums housing artifacts from various historical eras, and its connections to notable historical figures paint a vivid picture of a city steeped in culture and history. As visitors explore Parma's art, architecture, and traditions, they embark on a journey that reveals the profound impact of this remarkable city on the Italian Renaissance and its lasting legacy in the world of art and culture.

CHAPTER 10:

SAVOR THE LOCAL WINE SELECTION

Indulge In Tastings Of Regional Wines At Local Wineries

Parma, situated in the heart of Emilia-Romagna, is renowned not only for its culinary delights but also for its exceptional wines. The rolling hills surrounding the city are dotted with charming wineries that invite visitors to indulge in tastings of regional wines, each reflecting the unique terroir of the area. Engaging in wine tastings at local wineries is not just about sampling exquisite beverages; it's an immersive experience that combines the beauty of the landscape, the art of winemaking, and the warmth of local hospitality.

As you embark on a wine-tasting adventure in Parma, you'll find a variety of wineries, each with its own character and offerings. One notable winery is Cantine Pizzolato, located just outside of Parma. This family-run winery specializes in organic wines, showcasing their commitment to sustainable practices. A visit here typically includes a guided tour of the vineyards, where you'll learn about their organic farming techniques and the different grape varieties cultivated on the estate. The highlight, of course, is the tasting session, where you can sample their range of wines, including their acclaimed Sangiovese and Malvasia.

Another must-visit is Tenuta La Palazzina, renowned for its Lambrusco wines, which are a staple of the Emilia-Romagna region. This winery offers a beautiful setting with panoramic views of the vineyards. Their tastings often include a selection of sparkling and still Lambrusco, allowing visitors to appreciate the wine's versatility. A tour of Tenuta La Palazzina includes insights into the winemaking process, from grape harvest to fermentation. You'll have the chance to taste their signature Lambrusco Salamino, known for its deep red color and fruity notes, alongside light antipasti for a complete sensory experience.

Most wineries in the Parma area also offer a range of tasting packages, with options to include food pairings. Expect to pay around €15-€30 per person for a basic tasting, which often includes multiple wines and a small selection of local cheeses or cured meats. For a more elaborate experience, many wineries host special events, such as seasonal festivals or wine-and-dine evenings, where you can savor their wines alongside a gourmet meal prepared by local chefs.

To enhance your wine-tasting journey, consider booking a tour that combines visits to multiple wineries. This way, you can explore the diversity of Parma's wine scene, sampling everything from robust reds to refreshing whites. Local tour operators often provide transportation, which allows you to enjoy the tastings without the worry of driving. As a guideline, full-day wine tours typically cost between €100-€200 per person, depending on the inclusions, such as lunch and winery fees.

Learn About The Unique Characteristics Of Parma's Winemaking Process

Parma's winemaking process is deeply rooted in tradition, reflecting the rich agricultural heritage of the Emilia-Romagna region. The unique characteristics of Parma's wines can be attributed to several factors, including the region's climate, soil composition, and winemaking techniques. Understanding these elements will deepen your appreciation for the wines you taste and the stories behind them.

The climate in Parma is ideal for viticulture, characterized by hot summers and mild winters. This climatic condition allows grapes to ripen fully, developing robust flavors and sugars essential for quality wine. The fertile soil, rich in clay and limestone, also contributes to the distinctive flavor profiles of the wines produced in the area. Each winery typically employs sustainable farming practices, emphasizing the importance of preserving the land for future generations.

One of the standout features of winemaking in Parma is the use of indigenous grape varieties. While many people are familiar with Sangiovese and Lambrusco, other lesser-known varietals, such as Fortana and Barbera, are gaining recognition. These indigenous grapes thrive in the region's soil and climate, yielding wines that reflect the local terroir. For instance, Fortana is a unique grape variety that produces a light, fruity red wine, often enjoyed young, while Barbera offers a bolder flavor profile, making it ideal for aging.

The winemaking process itself varies among wineries but generally includes traditional methods passed down through generations. After harvesting, the grapes are carefully sorted to ensure only the best quality is used for fermentation. Many wineries in Parma practice spontaneous fermentation, where the natural yeast from the grape skins is allowed to initiate the fermentation process. This technique enhances the wine's complexity and character, making each bottle a true reflection of its origins.

Another significant aspect of winemaking in Parma is the aging process. Many wineries use a combination of stainless steel tanks and oak barrels for aging their wines. Stainless steel is often preferred for white wines, preserving their fresh and fruity flavors, while red wines typically benefit from aging in oak barrels, which imparts additional complexity and depth. The aging period can vary widely, with some wines aged for just a few months, while others mature for several years before being released.

In addition to traditional methods, some wineries in Parma are embracing innovative techniques and technology to enhance their winemaking. For instance, the use of temperature-controlled fermentation tanks allows winemakers to precisely manage the fermentation process, ensuring consistent quality year after year. This blend of tradition and modernity helps position Parma's wines as both classic and contemporary.

As you visit wineries, take the opportunity to ask about their specific winemaking techniques and philosophies. Many winemakers are passionate about sharing their knowledge and stories, offering insights that enrich your tasting experience. Learning about the unique characteristics of Parma's winemaking process not only enhances your appreciation for the wines but also deepens your connection to the land and its people.

Pair Wines With Local Cheeses For An Authentic Experience

Pairing wines with local cheeses is a delightful way to experience the culinary heritage of Parma. The region is famous for its artisanal cheeses, and the combination of wine and cheese creates a harmonious balance of flavors that showcases the best of both worlds. Engaging in wine and cheese pairings allows you to discover new taste sensations while enjoying the rich cultural traditions of Parma.

One of the most iconic cheeses to pair with Parma's wines is Parmigiano Reggiano. Known as the "King of Cheeses," this hard cheese has a nutty and savory flavor profile that complements a wide range of wines. When enjoying a glass of red Lambrusco, the effervescence of the wine cuts through the creaminess of the cheese, creating a delightful contrast. Alternatively, a crisp white wine, such as Malvasia, enhances the cheese's complex flavors, making for a refreshing pairing.

Many wineries offer specialized tasting experiences that include wine and cheese pairings. For instance, Cantina della Volta is known for its sparkling wines, and they often host events featuring local cheeses alongside their bubbly selections. During these tastings, knowledgeable staff will guide you through the pairing process, explaining the nuances of each wine and cheese combination. Expect to pay around €25-€50 for a tasting that includes several wine and cheese pairings, making it a memorable culinary experience.

In addition to Parmigiano Reggiano, other local cheeses worth exploring include Grana Padano, Gorgonzola, and Taleggio. Each cheese has its unique flavor profile and texture, providing a diverse range of pairing possibilities. Gorgonzola, with its creamy and tangy character, pairs beautifully with sweet dessert wines like Moscato. On the other hand, the strong flavor of Taleggio complements robust red wines such as Barbera or aged Sangiovese.

When visiting local markets, such as the Mercato di Parma, you can find a wide array of artisanal cheeses to take home or enjoy on the spot. Many vendors offer samples, allowing you to taste before you buy, and staff are often eager to recommend wine pairings. The market is open every day except Sunday, with peak hours on Wednesdays and Saturdays. Arriving early in the morning gives you the best selection and the chance to experience the lively atmosphere of locals shopping for their fresh produce and cheeses.

For a truly authentic experience, consider participating in a cheese-making workshop at a local dairy. Some farms around Parma offer hands-on experiences where you can learn about the cheese-making process, from milking the cows to curdling the milk and aging the cheese. These workshops typically last a few hours and may cost between €50-€100 per person, depending on the length and inclusions. The experience is not only educational but also delicious, as you get to sample the cheeses you've made, often paired with regional wines.

In summary, indulging in tastings of regional wines at local wineries, learning about the unique characteristics of Parma's winemaking process, and pairing wines with local cheeses for an authentic experience offers an enriching exploration of Parma's culinary scene. Engaging with the local winemakers and cheesemakers will deepen your appreciation for the traditions and techniques that define this remarkable region, creating unforgettable memories that linger long after your visit.

CHAPTER 11:

ENGAGE WITH LOCAL ARTISANS

Visit Workshops Where Skilled Artisans Create Traditional Crafts

Parma, a city celebrated for its rich history and culture, is also home to a vibrant artisan community that continues to preserve traditional crafts. Visitors have the opportunity to explore various workshops where skilled artisans showcase their expertise, offering a fascinating glimpse into the age-old techniques that define local craftsmanship. Immersing yourself in this world not only enriches your travel experience but also connects you to the heart and soul of Parma's cultural heritage.

As you wander through the streets of Parma, you'll discover workshops tucked away in charming corners, each specializing in unique crafts. One of the most notable artisan crafts in the region is pottery. At Ceramiche Nove, a family-run pottery studio, visitors can observe artisans as they skillfully mold clay into intricate pieces. Here, traditional techniques are blended with contemporary designs, resulting in beautiful ceramics that reflect the spirit of Parma. Workshops at Ceramiche Nove often welcome visitors for hands-on experiences, allowing you to try your hand at pottery making under the guidance of experienced artisans. Expect to create your own piece to take home, making for a memorable keepsake from your visit.

Another traditional craft worth exploring is textile weaving, showcased at Laboratorio di Tessitura, a workshop dedicated to preserving the art of weaving. The artisans here create exquisite textiles using looms, often employing patterns that have been passed down through generations. Visitors are encouraged to participate in weaving demonstrations and learn about the different techniques and materials used. The workshop also offers a selection of handmade textiles for sale, from scarves to table runners, providing you with unique souvenirs that embody the rich textile heritage of Parma.

In addition to pottery and textiles, Parma is renowned for its craftsmanship in parchment and bookbinding. The Bottega di Calzolaio specializes in handcrafted leather goods, where skilled artisans meticulously craft items ranging from shoes to wallets. Here, visitors can watch as leather is dyed, cut, and stitched to create beautiful products that are both functional and artistic. The workshop also offers personalized items, allowing you to select designs and initials to make your souvenir even more special.

As you explore these workshops, take the time to engage with the artisans. Their passion for their craft is infectious, and many are eager to share stories about their techniques and the history behind their work. This interaction provides a deeper understanding of the significance of craftsmanship in Parma's culture. The skills that artisans cultivate over years of practice are not merely trades; they represent a connection to the past and a commitment to preserving traditions for future generations.

Learn About The Importance Of Craftsmanship In Parma's Culture

The importance of craftsmanship in Parma's culture cannot be overstated. It is a reflection of the city's identity and a vital component of its heritage. The artisan community in Parma is deeply rooted in tradition, with many crafts being practiced for centuries. This dedication to craftsmanship has fostered a sense of pride among locals, who value the skills and artistry that go into creating handmade products.

Craftsmanship in Parma is often linked to the concept of "saper fare," which translates to "knowing how to do." This philosophy emphasizes the importance of skills and knowledge passed down through generations. Artisans take great pride in their work, often viewing it as a form of storytelling, where each piece embodies the history, culture, and values of the region. For instance, the intricate designs found in ceramics often reflect local landscapes, while textile patterns may draw inspiration from historical motifs.

The revival of interest in traditional crafts has been fueled by a growing appreciation for handmade goods and the value of supporting local artisans. Visitors to Parma can see firsthand how these crafts contribute to the economy and cultural landscape. Many workshops offer internships and apprenticeships, ensuring that the skills are passed on to younger generations. This commitment to education and skill-building is crucial for preserving the heritage of Parma's craftsmanship.

Moreover, craftsmanship plays a vital role in promoting sustainable practices. Many artisans prioritize using local materials and traditional methods that are environmentally friendly. By sourcing materials locally, artisans support the local economy while reducing their carbon footprint. This focus on sustainability resonates with travelers seeking authentic experiences that align with their values.

As you immerse yourself in the world of Parma's artisans, you'll likely encounter various events and festivals celebrating craftsmanship. The Festa dell'Artigianato, held annually in the city, showcases local artisans and their work. Visitors can browse stalls, attend demonstrations, and participate in workshops, providing a unique opportunity to engage with the artisan community. Events like these highlight the significance of craftsmanship in Parma, creating a vibrant atmosphere that fosters appreciation for handmade goods.

Furthermore, the recognition of craftsmanship extends beyond the local level. Many artisans in Parma have gained international acclaim for their work, participating in exhibitions and craft fairs around the world. This exposure not only elevates their craft but also puts Parma on the map as a hub for traditional and contemporary artisanship. By supporting these artisans during your visit, you contribute to the preservation of their craft and the promotion of their stories to a global audience.

Take Home Unique Souvenirs That Reflect The Local Artistry

One of the most rewarding aspects of exploring the artisan community in Parma is the opportunity to take home unique souvenirs that reflect the local artistry. These handcrafted items not only serve as tangible reminders of your travels but also carry the essence of Parma's rich cultural heritage. When selecting souvenirs, consider the stories and craftsmanship behind each piece, making your purchase even more meaningful.

Handmade pottery is a popular choice among visitors. The vibrant colors and intricate designs of ceramics from Ceramiche Nove are perfect for adding a touch of Parma to your home. Consider purchasing a decorative bowl or a set of mugs that can be used for years to come. Each piece is unique, ensuring that you have a one-of-a-kind item that embodies the spirit of the region.

Textiles, such as handwoven scarves or table runners from Laboratorio di Tessitura, also make for exquisite souvenirs. These pieces are not only functional but also carry the artistry and tradition of the weavers. Opting for a textile item is a great way to support local artisans while acquiring something beautiful for your wardrobe or home decor. When you wear or display these textiles, you'll carry a piece of Parma's history with you.

For those interested in leather goods, a handcrafted wallet or handbag from Bottega di Calzolaio is an excellent option. The quality and craftsmanship of leather products from Parma are unmatched, and each item tells a story of skilled artisans pouring their heart and soul into their work. Personalized leather goods, featuring your initials or a unique design, make for a special souvenir that reflects your individuality.

In addition to these items, don't overlook the charm of locally produced food products. Many artisans create culinary delights, such as artisanal pasta, cheeses, and preserved goods. Visiting local markets allows you to sample these delicacies and select items to bring home. Imagine sharing a taste of Parma with friends and family, showcasing the flavors and craftsmanship of the region.

When purchasing souvenirs, it's essential to consider the impact of your choices. Opting for handmade items directly supports local artisans and helps sustain their crafts. Many artisans face challenges in competing with mass-produced goods, and your support can make a significant difference. Choosing unique, handcrafted souvenirs not only enriches your collection but also contributes to the preservation of Parma's artistic heritage.

As you explore workshops and markets, take the time to connect with the artisans behind the products. They often have stories to share about their craft and the techniques used, making your shopping experience more personal and memorable. This connection adds another layer of meaning to your purchases, as you become part of their narrative.

In summary, visiting workshops where skilled artisans create traditional crafts, learning about the importance of craftsmanship in

Parma's culture, and taking home unique souvenirs that reflect the local artistry creates a rich and fulfilling experience. Engaging with artisans, understanding their stories, and supporting their crafts not only enhances your appreciation for the artistry but also connects you to the heart of Parma's vibrant culture. Whether you leave with a piece of pottery, a handwoven textile, or a bottle of locally produced delicacies, you carry with you the essence of Parma, making your journey truly unforgettable.

CHAPTER 12:

EXPLORE UNIQUE SHOPPING EXPERIENCES

Stroll Through Boutiques Offering Handmade Goods And Local Products

In the heart of Parma, a delightful array of boutiques beckons those with an appreciation for artisanal craftsmanship and local products. Strolling through these charming shops, visitors are treated to a unique shopping experience that goes beyond the typical souvenir hunt. Here, handmade goods crafted by skilled artisans reflect the rich cultural heritage of the region, making for perfect keepsakes or gifts that carry a story.

As you embark on your boutique exploration, consider beginning at La Bottega dei Sapori, a quaint shop that specializes in gourmet foods and local delicacies. Here, you'll find an impressive selection of regional products, including Parmigiano Reggiano, a cheese that embodies the flavors of the area. The knowledgeable staff is eager to share samples, helping you choose the best varieties to take home. Pricing for Parmigiano Reggiano can range from $15 to $30 per kilogram, depending on the aging process. This cheese is not only a staple in Italian cuisine but also a culinary treasure that reflects the passion and skill of local cheesemakers.

Next, make your way to Artigianato del Colore, a boutique dedicated to showcasing local artisans' creations. This shop features handmade textiles, from vibrant tablecloths to stylish scarves, all crafted using traditional techniques. The colorful fabrics often showcase motifs inspired by the surrounding landscapes, making them a perfect way to bring a piece of Parma into your home. Prices for handcrafted textiles typically start at around $30 for smaller items, ensuring that there's something for every budget.

For those interested in home décor, Ceramiche del Castello offers a stunning array of hand-painted ceramics. Each piece is a work of art, with intricate designs that celebrate the region's history and culture.

From dinnerware to decorative tiles, these ceramics serve as both functional items and beautiful décor. A typical ceramic plate may range from $20 to $50, depending on the size and complexity of the design. Purchasing these items not only supports local artists but also allows you to bring a unique slice of Parma into your daily life.

As you wander through the boutiques, take the time to chat with the shop owners and artisans. They are often passionate about their work and eager to share the stories behind their creations. This personal connection enhances the shopping experience, making it more memorable. Many boutiques also offer workshops where you can learn to create your own handmade goods, such as pottery or textiles. These experiences typically cost around $50 to $100, depending on the materials and duration, allowing you to leave with not just a product, but also skills to create something of your own.

Continuing your stroll, don't miss Bottega della Moda, a boutique specializing in fashion accessories. Here, you can find unique handmade jewelry crafted from local materials, each piece telling its own story. Prices for artisan jewelry generally range from $25 to $100, offering something for every taste and budget. Many pieces are inspired by the natural beauty of the Emilia-Romagna region, making them perfect gifts for loved ones or a treat for yourself.

Exploring the boutiques of Parma provides a glimpse into the local culture, revealing the craftsmanship and creativity that thrive within the community. Each item purchased carries with it the essence of Parma, making it a cherished reminder of your travels. Whether you choose a gourmet delicacy, a piece of textile, or a handcrafted accessory, you'll be taking home a piece of Parma's artistic soul.

Discover Artisan Markets Featuring Fresh Produce And Crafts

No visit to Parma would be complete without immersing yourself in the vibrant artisan markets that showcase the region's fresh produce and handmade crafts. These markets are a feast for the senses, filled with colorful stalls, the aroma of fresh ingredients, and the sounds of lively conversations among locals and visitors alike. They provide a perfect opportunity to connect with the community and discover the authentic flavors and crafts that define Parma.

One of the most popular markets in the area is the Mercato di Parma, held every Saturday morning in the historic city center. This bustling market is a local favorite, offering an impressive selection of fresh fruits, vegetables, cheeses, meats, and baked goods. Here, you can engage with farmers and producers, learning about their practices and the origins of their products. Prices for fresh produce are generally reasonable, with seasonal fruits and vegetables averaging around $2 to $4 per kilogram. Be sure to try local specialties, such as torta fritta, a delicious fried pastry often paired with cured meats like Prosciutto di Parma.

In addition to fresh produce, the Mercato di Parma features stalls selling handmade crafts, including artisanal soaps, pottery, and textiles.

Each vendor takes pride in their creations, providing an opportunity for visitors to purchase unique items directly from the artisans. For example, a handmade ceramic mug may cost around $15, while a bar of artisanal soap could be priced at $5. Supporting local artisans not only enriches your shopping experience but also helps sustain traditional crafts in the region.

Another must-visit market is the Fiera di San Giovanni, held annually in late June. This festival celebrates local artisans and their crafts, showcasing a diverse range of handmade goods. From leather products to handcrafted jewelry, the market attracts artisans from all over the region. Visitors can also enjoy live music, street performances, and delicious food stalls, making it a festive occasion for all. Prices for items at this market can vary widely, with small crafts starting around $10 and larger, more intricate pieces reaching upwards of $100.

For those looking for a unique experience, consider visiting the Mercato della Terra, a farmer's market focused on organic and sustainable products. Held monthly, this market features local farmers and producers committed to environmentally friendly practices. Here, you'll find an array of organic fruits and vegetables, free-range meats, and artisanal cheeses. Prices may be slightly higher than at conventional markets, with organic produce averaging $3 to $6 per kilogram, but the quality and flavor are well worth the investment.

As you explore these artisan markets, take time to sample local delicacies. Many vendors offer tastings, allowing you to experience the flavors of Parma firsthand. Be sure to try Prosciutto di Parma, the region's famous cured ham, known for its rich flavor and delicate texture. A typical price for a good quality Prosciutto can range from $20 to $40 per kilogram, depending on the aging process.

Engaging with local vendors at the markets not only enhances your experience but also helps you understand the significance of food and crafts in Parma's culture. Many vendors are happy to share recipes, cooking tips, and stories about their products, making your visit even more enriching. Purchasing goods directly from the artisans and farmers fosters a sense of community and connection, ensuring that your shopping experience is both meaningful and memorable.

Find Perfect Gifts That Capture The Essence Of Parma

Finding the perfect gifts that capture the essence of Parma is an exciting aspect of your visit, allowing you to share the city's unique culture and craftsmanship with friends and family back home. As you explore the boutiques and artisan markets, keep an eye out for items that not only reflect Parma's rich heritage but also offer a glimpse into the lives of the artisans who create them.

Handmade food products make for excellent gifts, showcasing the flavors of Parma. Consider purchasing a beautifully packaged selection of Parmigiano Reggiano, along with a bottle of local balsamic vinegar. These items can typically be found at markets and specialty shops, with prices for quality cheese starting at around $20 per kilogram and premium balsamic vinegar costing between $15 to $30 for a bottle. Together, they create a delightful gift set that embodies the culinary delights of the region.

Another thoughtful gift idea is a selection of artisanal pasta, such as tagliatelle or tortellini. Many local shops offer beautifully packaged pasta, often made using traditional methods. A package of handcrafted pasta can be priced around $5 to $10, making it an affordable and authentic gift. Pair it with a jar of homemade sauce or pesto, available at markets, for a complete Italian meal experience that your loved ones will appreciate.

For those interested in handcrafted goods, consider picking up a piece of local pottery or ceramics. A unique bowl or decorative plate from Ceramiche del Castello not only serves as a functional item but also adds a touch of Parma's artistic heritage to any home. Prices for ceramics typically range from $20 to $50, making them accessible gifts that carry the essence of the region. These items often feature intricate designs and vibrant colors, ensuring that they stand out as memorable keepsakes.

Artisan jewelry also makes for a cherished gift. A handcrafted necklace or bracelet from local boutiques showcases the craftsmanship and creativity of Parma's artisans. With prices starting around $25, you can find beautiful pieces that cater to various styles, from delicate designs to bold statements. Gifting artisan jewelry allows you to share a piece of Parma's culture while supporting local craftsmanship.

If you're looking for something more personal, consider custom-made items. Many artisans offer the option to personalize their creations, such as engraving names or initials on leather goods or textiles. This thoughtful touch elevates the gift, making it a special memento that recipients will treasure. The cost for personalized items can vary, but expect to pay an additional $10 to $30 for customization.

Finally, don't overlook the beauty of local artworks. Purchasing a small painting or print from an artisan at one of the markets or galleries can be a meaningful way to bring a piece of Parma home. Art can range in price significantly, with smaller pieces starting around $30 and larger, more intricate works going up to several hundred dollars. Each piece tells a story and carries the spirit of Parma, making it a unique and heartfelt gift.

In conclusion, strolling through boutiques offering handmade goods and local products, discovering artisan markets featuring fresh produce and crafts, and finding perfect gifts that capture the essence of Parma create an enriching travel experience. Engaging with local artisans, sampling delicious foods, and selecting unique items to take home allows you to connect with the culture and spirit of this beautiful city. Whether it's a delicious culinary treat, a piece of handcrafted pottery, or a vibrant textile, each purchase you make is a reflection of Parma's rich heritage, ensuring that your memories of this enchanting destination last long after your visit.

CHAPTER 13:

YOUR 6-DAY ADVENTURE AWAITS

A well-crafted itinerary to make the most of your stay in Parma

Welcome to your ultimate 6-day tour itinerary of Parma, a city steeped in history, culture, and culinary delights. Whether you're an art enthusiast, a food lover, or someone simply looking to soak up the charming atmosphere of this enchanting Italian city, this guide will help you navigate through the best that Parma has to offer. Each day is packed with a mix of activities that will allow you to explore the city's rich heritage, indulge in its famous cuisine, and immerse yourself in the warm hospitality of its people. From visiting stunning historical landmarks and picturesque parks to enjoying local delicacies and discovering artisan shops, this itinerary will guide you through a balanced blend of relaxation and adventure. So, get ready to embrace the beauty and flavors of Parma as we embark on this unforgettable journey together!

Day 1: Arrival in Parma and Exploring the Historic Center

Your first day in Parma should be spent getting acquainted with the city's historic center, which is a UNESCO World Heritage site. After settling into your accommodation, start your exploration at the Piazza della Pace, a lively square surrounded by some of Parma's most important landmarks. Here, you'll find the Palazzo della Pilotta, a grand palace housing the National Gallery and the Teatro Farnese, a stunning wooden theater that is a must-see. Spend the morning wandering through the gallery, admiring masterpieces by renowned artists such as Correggio and Parmigianino.

For lunch, make your way to a local trattoria, where you can indulge in tortelli d'erbetta, a delicious pasta dish filled with herbs and served with melted butter and sage. This traditional dish perfectly embodies the flavors of Parma and is sure to delight your palate. After lunch, head to the Cattedrale di Parma and the adjacent Baptistery, both iconic symbols of the city's rich ecclesiastical heritage. Take your time to appreciate the intricate architecture and stunning frescoes that adorn these historic buildings.

In the late afternoon, take a leisurely stroll through the Giardini Ducali, a beautiful park that offers a peaceful retreat from the bustling city. Relax on a bench and soak in the tranquil atmosphere, or explore the gardens' winding paths. As the sun begins to set, find a cozy restaurant for dinner where you can sample Prosciutto di Parma, one of the region's most famous delicacies, paired with a glass of local wine. After dinner, wander back to your accommodation, reflecting on your first day in this charming city.

Day 2: Culinary Delights and Local Markets
Begin your day with breakfast at a local café, enjoying a cappuccino and a slice of torta fritta, a delicious fried pastry often served with cured meats. After fueling up, head to the Mercato di Parma, which takes place every Saturday in the historic city center. Here, you can browse stalls overflowing with fresh produce, cheeses, meats, and artisanal products. Take your time to sample local specialties, and don't hesitate to chat with the

vendors about their goods. This market is an excellent place to immerse yourself in the local culture and discover the region's culinary treasures.

After the market, consider signing up for a cooking class where you can learn to make traditional dishes, such as gnocchi or lasagna. Many local chefs offer classes that include a guided market tour followed by hands-on cooking lessons. This immersive experience usually costs around $80 and lasts a few hours, culminating in a delicious meal that you've prepared yourself.

In the afternoon, visit the Museo di Capodimonte to explore its impressive collection of art, particularly the works of Parmigianino. Take your time to wander through the exhibits, absorbing the beauty of the paintings. Following your museum visit, head to Bottega di Parma, a delightful shop where you can purchase local food products. Here, you can find various gourmet items, such as aged balsamic vinegar and handmade pasta, perfect for taking a piece of Parma home with you.

For dinner, consider dining at Ristorante Gallo d'Oro, where you can savor dishes made from locally sourced ingredients. Don't forget to try the tortellini in brodo, a traditional pasta dish served in broth, which is a true staple of Parma cuisine. After dinner, take a leisurely evening stroll through the illuminated streets of the historic center, admiring the charming architecture and vibrant atmosphere.

Day 3: Art and Culture in Parma
On your third day, immerse yourself in Parma's rich artistic heritage. Start your morning at the Teatro Regio, one of Italy's most prestigious opera houses. If time permits, consider taking a guided tour to learn about the theater's fascinating history and architecture. After the tour, make your way to the Galleria Nazionale di Parma, which houses an impressive collection of Renaissance art. Allocate a couple of hours to explore the gallery's masterpieces, including works by artists such as Correggio and Titian.

For lunch, head to Osteria dei Mascalzoni, where you can indulge in traditional Emilia-Romagna cuisine. Try their bollito misto, a mixed boiled meat dish served with various sauces, a regional favorite that will leave you satisfied and ready for more exploration.

In the afternoon, visit the Basilica di Santa Maria della Steccata, known for its stunning frescoes and intricate architecture. Afterward, take some time to explore the charming streets surrounding the basilica, filled with boutiques and artisan shops. Look for unique souvenirs, such as handmade ceramics or artisanal jewelry, that capture the essence of Parma.

As the sun sets, treat yourself to a wine tasting experience at one of the local wineries. Many offer guided tastings paired with light appetizers, allowing you to sample some of the region's renowned wines, such as Lambrusco or Malvasia. This experience typically costs around $30 to $50 per person and provides a lovely way to unwind after a day of exploration. For dinner, find a cozy trattoria and enjoy a pasta dish accompanied by a glass of local wine, reflecting on the day's cultural discoveries.

Day 4: Day Trip to the Countryside

On your fourth day, take a day trip to the beautiful Emilia-Romagna countryside. Rent a car or join a guided tour to explore the stunning landscapes dotted with vineyards, charming villages, and historical landmarks. Your first stop could be the picturesque village of Collecchio, known for its beautiful views and traditional architecture. Stroll through the village, and perhaps stop for a coffee at a local café to take in the serene atmosphere.

Next, head to Vignola, renowned for its cherry trees and beautiful castle. Visit the Rocca di Vignola, a medieval fortress offering breathtaking views of the surrounding countryside. The entrance fee is typically around $5, and the castle's rich history will transport you back in time.

For lunch, stop at a local agriturismo, where you can savor traditional Emilia-Romagna dishes prepared with fresh, locally sourced ingredients. Enjoy the hearty flavors of lasagna verde or crescente, a type of savory pie, paired with a glass of local wine.

After lunch, continue your journey to Modena, famous for its balsamic vinegar. Visit a traditional acetaia (balsamic vinegar factory) to learn about the production process and sample various types of balsamic vinegar. This experience typically lasts around an hour and costs around $10, providing insights into one of the region's most prized culinary products.

On your way back to Parma, consider stopping at Sassuolo, known for its stunning ceramic tile production. Explore the local shops and perhaps pick up some unique tiles or pottery as souvenirs. As the day winds down, return to Parma and enjoy a relaxed dinner at a restaurant of your choice, perhaps trying some gorgonzola or another local cheese as part of your meal.

Day 5: Nature and Relaxation
On your fifth day, take a break from the city's hustle and bustle and spend a day in nature. Start your day with a visit to the Parco Ducale, a beautiful park in the heart of Parma. Here, you can stroll through manicured gardens, relax by the ponds, and admire the grandiose

Ducal Palace. The park is a great place to unwind, and you might even come across locals practicing tai chi or jogging along the paths.

After enjoying the park, make your way to the Giardino della Ghiara, another stunning green space that offers a tranquil escape. This garden is home to various plant species and beautiful sculptures, making it an ideal spot for a leisurely afternoon. Consider bringing a picnic lunch with you, perhaps consisting of local cheeses, meats, and bread, which you can enjoy amidst the natural beauty.

In the afternoon, engage in outdoor activities, such as cycling or hiking in the surrounding countryside. There are several scenic trails near Parma, and renting a bicycle is a fantastic way to explore the area. Many local rental shops offer bikes for around $15 to $25 per day. As you ride through the rolling hills and vineyards, you'll appreciate the stunning landscapes that Emilia-Romagna has to offer.
For dinner, return to Parma and treat yourself to a leisurely meal at a restaurant known for its fresh seafood. Savor dishes like branzino

or spaghetti alle vongole, perfectly complemented by a crisp white wine. After dinner, take a leisurely stroll along the Taro River, enjoying the peaceful ambiance and the sound of water flowing.

Day 6: Artisans and Farewell to Parma
On your final day in Parma, dedicate your time to exploring the city's artisan scene. Start your morning by visiting local workshops where skilled artisans create traditional crafts. From handmade leather goods to intricate ceramics, you'll find a range of unique products that reflect Parma's artistic heritage. Many artisans are happy to share their techniques and stories, allowing you to gain a deeper appreciation for their work.

Next, visit Artisan Markets, where you can browse fresh produce, handmade crafts, and unique gifts. These markets are often bustling with activity, and you'll have the opportunity to interact with local vendors and learn about their products. As you explore, keep an eye out for perfect gifts to take home that capture the essence of Parma.

For lunch, find a local café and enjoy a light meal while reminiscing about your unforgettable journey through Parma. After lunch, take some time to revisit any favorite spots or do some last-minute shopping. You may want to explore the Via D'Azeglio, a charming street lined with boutiques and cafés, offering a perfect blend of local products and souvenirs.

As your time in Parma comes to an end, consider indulging in one final treat. Stop by a local gelateria to sample traditional Italian gelato. Enjoying a cone of rich stracciatella or refreshing limone will provide a sweet ending to your visit.

Finally, take a moment to reflect on the experiences you've had in this beautiful city. From its stunning architecture and rich history to its delicious cuisine and warm hospitality, Parma has surely left an imprint on your heart. Whether you're savoring the flavors of traditional dishes or wandering through picturesque streets, the memories you've created during this 6-day journey will stay with you long after you've returned home. As you depart, take with you not just souvenirs but the essence of Parma—a vibrant tapestry of art, culture, and gastronomy that will continue to inspire your future travels.

Printed in Great Britain
by Amazon